MILNER CRAFT SERIES

Original Designs for Silk Ribbon Embroidery

JENNY BRADFORD

SALLY MILNER PUBLISHING

First published in 1991 by
Sally Milner Publishing Pty Ltd
PO Box 2104
Bowral NSW 2576 Australia.

Reprinted 1992 (twice), 1993, 1994, 1999

© Jenny Bradford, 1991

Design by David Constable
Layout by Gatya Kelly, Doric Order
Illustrations by Don Bradford
Photography by Andre Martin
Typeset in Australia by Asset Typesetting Pty Ltd
Printed in Australia by Impact Printing, Melbourne

National Library of Australia Cataloguing-in-Publication data:

Bradford, Jenny, 1936-
    Original designs for silk ribbon embroidery.

    ISBN 1 86351 237 3

    1 .Embroidery – Patterns. 2. Ribbon work. I. Title.
    (Series : Milner craft series).

746.44041

ACKNOWLEDGEMENTS

I would like to thank the many needlewomen I meet throughout the year for their constant interest, enthusiasm and encouragement, without which this book would never have been written.

Special thanks to Chris Bromfield for making the lovely nightdress for me, and to my husband Don, whose contribution has been greater than ever before. As well as his meticulous attention to detail in the drawings and in proof reading, so necessary to ensure that the instructions are easily understood, Don has also taken over the typing of the manuscript.

I am once again indebted to Veronica Henry of Cotton On Creations, Mittagong, NSW, for donating all the silk ribbon, threads, lace and fabric used for working the samples for this book.

My grateful thanks to Luxo Australia of Brookvale, NSW for supplying me with the perfect answer to poor lighting and imperfect eyesight.

To Ireland Needlecraft of Ashwood, Victoria, for donating the Framecraft brooch mounts and a Sudbury House tray, to Needlecraft International, Eastwood, NSW, for the handbag frame and pattern and DD Creative Crafts, Ringwood, Victoria, for perforated paper, all of which were used in preparing samples for this book, my grateful thanks.

Jenny Bradford 1991

CONTENTS

INTRODUCTION

E ach of the previous three books I have written on silk ribbon embroidery was based on a different set of stitches suitable for ribbon work. I felt that it was important to expand the range of stitches to add variety to this fascinating form of embroidery.

This book expands the field of silk ribbon embroidery using the stitches and techniques detailed in those earlier publications. New ways of using the stitches are introduced, together with new designs and projects, to widen the field even further.

All the stitches that I have used in my ribbon embroidery books are contained in a glossary at the back of this book, making it a useful reference book for the enthusiast.

Instead of detailing the basic techniques for working with silk ribbon yet again, this information is contained in the first chapter 'How do you get it to look like that?'

Once again new flowers are detailed with a mixture of cottage garden flowers together with some new Australian wildflowers. For me the most exciting work has come from developing new ways of working butterflies and lettering. This wide field will add interest and variety to the art of silk ribbon embroidery. By expanding the design of the charted butterfly featured in *Silk Ribbon Embroidery for Gifts and Garments*, more ideas for tiny charted designs have been created; I have also explored the possibilities of working much larger butterflies using straight stitch in a variety of ways.

Finally, as always I have tried to include many ideas for using the designs, and full size detailed patterns are given for all the work featured in the colour plates, except where embroidery is shown on garments. A chapter on embroidery on clothing will assist readers in choosing styles and garments to suit their own requirements.

CHAPTER ONE

'HOW DO YOU GET IT TO LOOK LIKE THAT?'

T his is the comment most frequently made to me in workshops and at the many shows I attend throughout the year. In this section I will deal with the questions I am most frequently asked, as they indicate to me the problems people have when handling the ribbon. The explanations are usually very simple. In most cases they are necessary because I find students learning the art of ribbon embroidery have, in their enthusiasm to get to the actual project, failed to appreciate the importance of the basic techniques of manipulating the ribbon.

It is all too easy to rush over chapters on basic technique in our enthusiasm to get on with the task. How many times are we all reminded of the saying 'when all else fails read the instructions'. Our hectic lifestyle and lack of time seem to make this almost a daily cry. However, if we make the effort to master the basics thoroughly it does save time and effort in the long run.

As with any specialised field, the 'tools of the trade' and working conditions are extremely important. The degree of involvement will generally dictate the amount of investment you will need to make in equipment.

It is important to pay attention to the various types of needles and embroidery hoops recommended. Only pure silk ribbon will give results similar to those depicted in the photographs.

Having considered these factors, give careful thought to good lighting and clear vision. For me the best answer is a Luxo Examiner K Mag lamp as photographed. The fluorescent lamp gives a cool light (no hot and sweaty hands) and the magnified area is excellent. The lamp is easily adjusted to give a comfortable working position. A cheaper alternative is another Luxo lamp, the Argus-1, which is very good except for the heat radiated by the incandescent bulb; but that is not always a problem. There are also many portable magnifying glasses available from needlwork shops or opticians and these can be utilised together with a good lamp.

Further detailed instructions of all the techniques mentioned in this chapter may be found in any one of my earlier books on silk ribbon embroidery.

Q1. 'WHAT FABRIC CAN I USE?'

The main factors to be considered when choosing fabric for your project are:

- The less you have to iron silk ribbon embroidery the better. The embroidery will retain its original form if the background fabric does not require excessive ironing. This is very important when choosing fabric for a garment which will need constant laundering. (See Q2.)

- The ribbon will be easier to work on a fabric with a weave that is not too loose or too tight. Fabric such as taffeta has a very dense weave and may need special consideration. (See Q6 & Q7.)

- Knitted fabrics often have too loose a weave to hold the ribbon securely. This problem can be overcome by backing the area to be embroidered with a very fine non-stretch fabric such as voile or silk organza.

My favourite fabrics include raw or noil silk, although this is, unfortunately, very hard to obtain in any colour other than cream. Most dressmaking fabrics, including silks, synthetics and good quality homespun, cottons, voile and batiste, are suitable. (See Q3.)

Regular evenweave embroidery fabrics such as lugana, linda and hardanger 22 are also easy to use.

One word of warning. Do remember that the fabric you choose has to be washed according to the most delicate fibres, which usually relates to the silk ribbon. (See Q2.) For example, using a towel as a base for ribbon embroidery is not a good idea. A towel normally requires the use of stronger detergent and hotter water than you would use on silk fibres.

Q2. 'IS RIBBON EMBROIDERY WASHABLE AND COLOURFAST?'

The answer to this is 'Yes' in most cases. The embroidery should of course be treated the way you would wash any other form of silk fabric. Use a suitable solution for delicate fabrics and wash by hand or on a delicate cycle in your washing machine.

Some stitches do wash more successfully than others and the general guide is that the more firmly knotted or twisted the stitch the better it will stand up to washing and wearing. It is therefore wise to choose appropriate stitches and flowers etc. that fall into this category for garments and other projects that will have hard use. (See the stitch glossary for the stitches to use.)

Most of the ribbons are colourfast; however, I have found some of the strong colours — deep reds, purple, blue and black may colour-leak a little. There is no problem if you use these colours on a dark background; but I do recommend care when selecting colours for use on pale backgrounds if you do not wish to go to the expense of having the item dry cleaned.

If you do have ribbon embroidery dry cleaned I suggest that you ask that they do not press the item and always make sure that the dry cleaners are aware that silk has been used for the embroidery. (See Q1.)

Q3. 'SHOULD I USE A BACKING ON MY FABRIC?'

Although not always necessary, I use a backing of fine pellon on my fabric whenever I can; I do this for the following reasons:

- It helps to keep the surface fabric smooth and makes the mounting process of the finished work easier.
- It ensures that the ribbon ends left on the back of the work do not show through to the front, especially if the surface fabric is very fine, for example, voile or batiste.
- It helps to minimise the marks left by using an embroidery hoop.

When working on clothing, the use of pellon is not always practical, but it is sometimes possible to use a second layer of fabric for the same purpose.

When working on stretch fabrics the embroidery will sit more evenly if you back the area with a fine non-stretch fabric such as voile or silk organza. This enables the work area to be mounted in a hoop and holds the ribbon in place more securely.

Q4. 'DO I HAVE TO USE A HOOP?'

This varies according to the type of work being done, but in the majority of cases a hoop is essential if you are going to manipulate the ribbon correctly and produce good even work.

As with all hand work, it is personal pleasure and satisfaction that is the most important thing. It is essential that you are comfortable working and are also producing work of a standard that gives you a feeling of personal satisfaction.

Some of the outline stitches are easy to work without a hoop if the background fabric is firm enough not to crease and pucker (see Q3) and if it is not necessary to spread the ribbon.

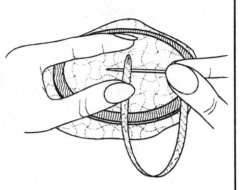

Stitches where 'spreading the ribbon' is vital require the fabric to be held really taut and therefore the use of a hoop is strongly recommended.

My preference is to use the smallest hoop possible and, with careful planning, I find that a 3″ or 3½″ (8 or 9 cm) plastic frame hoop the best for most projects. The frame is thin, allowing the hoop to be balanced in the left hand, resting on the second, third and fourth fingers. This enables you to use the thumb and first finger of the left hand on top of the fabric for manipulating the ribbon.

The gap in the wire section of the frame is useful for passing some of the work through without it being clamped into the frame and crushing your work.

When using a large hoop, support it comfortably on the edge of a table and work with a second needle to spread and control the ribbon rather than trying to use your fingers.

Q5. 'WHAT TYPE OF NEEDLE SHOULD I USE?'

There is no broad, simple answer to this question. It is very important to use the right type and size of needle for the selected stitch.

In general, you require an assortment of tapestry needles (broad eye, blunt point), chenille needles (large eye, thick shaft, sharp point) and crewel needles (slender eye, thin shaft, sharp point). The size of the needle chosen depends on several factors. (See Q6.)

A guide to the type of needle recommended for the various stitches is included in the stitch glossary.

Q6. 'IS THE SIZE OF THE NEEDLE IMPORTANT?'

Yes! Selecting the correct sized needle for your work is the most important decision of all.

The wrong choice is often made because we are taught, in general, to use the finest needle possible for all embroidery. This is definitely not the case where ribbon embroidery is concerned.

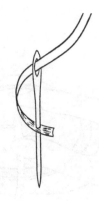

• The size of the needle required varies in direct proportion to the density of the weave of the fabric you choose to work on. In general, the tighter the weave the *larger* the needle. (See Q7.)

The needle should puncture a hole in the fabric large enough for the ribbon to pass through easily and spread out sufficiently for the stitch to be worked smoothly. (See Q7 & Q8.) This can often lead to the feeling that you are using a 'crow bar' and are going to leave unsightly holes in the fabric. However, the fact that the ribbon works easily this way and looks so much better soon overcomes this concern.

In general, I use a size 22 tapestry or chenille needle for most of my work. Thread the needle as shown in the diagram to avoid losing it off the end of the ribbon.

Q7. 'WHY DOES THE RIBBON FRAY?'

Silk ribbon is delicate and if it is over-stressed in use it will deteriorate quickly.

The main cause of fraying is the use of too *small* a needle. (See Q6.) The size of the needle must be adjusted so that it makes a hole large enough for the ribbon to pass through the base fabric easily, without causing friction on the ribbon.

If the base fabric is hard or stiff it may be abrasive and cause stress on the ribbon. If this is the case, try washing the fabric, using a fabric softener, prior to use.

The ribbon will deteriorate if over-worked, which can occur if too long a piece is threaded in the needle. Short lengths are easier to manipulate and quicker to work with. Approximately 30 cm (12″) lengths are ideal.

Q8. 'WHY DO MY STITCHES LOOK SO THIN AND SKINNY?'

This can be due to two factors. Failing to 'spread the ribbon' before completing each stitch is generally the major problem.

Spreading the ribbon successfully is crucial to forming stitches that show the full width of the ribbon.

Choosing the right sized needle is the most important thing to ensure the ribbon spreads. You *must* make a hole large enough for the ribbon to open out as it passes through the hole. If this is done the creases will even

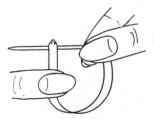

out neatly as the process of spreading the ribbon is completed. This involves holding the ribbon firmly under the left thumb as you run the needle under the ribbon back towards the point of exit, pulling up on the needle as you work, as shown in the diagram.

If this does not produce the required result, turn the ribbon over and repeat the process, as it may have twisted as it passed through the fabric. You will soon learn what to look for and when further adjustment is required. It is very important to get it right at this stage to avoid any temptation to poke the stitch around once it is completed.

The second factor that affects the look of the stitches is tension. Ribbon work is delicate and a very delicate touch is required to achieve just the right tension. Pulling a stitch a fraction too tight will result in the stitch losing its form and fullness. This usually happens only when working straight or ribbon stitch.

The best way to avoid this problem is to brace your hand against the underside of the hoop as you complete the stitch and work the ribbon down *very gently* until the correct look is achieved. Should you accidentally pull a straight stitch too tight, don't panic; you can rectify the situation by working a second stitch directly over the top, instead of unpicking the mistake.

Q9. 'How do I prevent the ribbon twisting as I work?'

- Use short lengths to work with (see Q7).
- Make sure you have paid attention to the technique discussed in Q6.
- Learn to manipulate the ribbon by holding the flat, untwisted ribbon under the left thumb as the needle is pulled to the back of the work. Pull the loop firmly around the thumb and the twists should pass through the fabric before the thumb is removed, leaving a smooth, flat loop with which to form the stitch. (See diagram).

An alternative to this method is to work the loop over a second needle held in the left hand. (Use a large tapestry needle to avoid snagging the ribbon). Tension the loop as you work by pulling up firmly with the second needle as the first needle is pulled to the back of the work. (See diagram.)

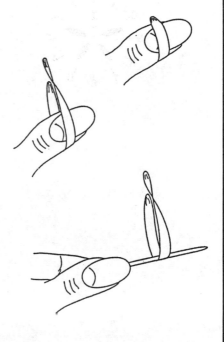

I cannot stress enough how important it is to perfect at least one of these alternatives and thus master the process of forming the stitches without having to prod at them once they are laid down on the fabric. Trying to re-adjust ribbon work usually results in the ribbon being snagged and not looking any better at all.

Q10. 'HOW DO I GET EVEN SPACING WHEN I WORK A FLOWER?'

Even numbers of petals generally make spacing a fairly easy process. For flowers such as daisies with many petals it is easier to put in four key petals first (see 3A on the sampler) and then fill in between these. This method also helps to keep the petals radiating evenly from the centre of the flower.

Five petal flowers are more difficult and it is essential to have a clear picture in your mind of what you are aiming to do. I prefer to mark the centre of the flower only and therefore suggest the use of any of the following images to help my students create that clear picture.

- Picture a Y and work three petals in this formation. Position the fourth and fifth petals in the spaces.
- Imagine a stick figure as drawn for a child with a head, two arms and two legs.
- Imagine the centre of the flower is a clock face and work petals as shown on the diagram.

Choose the image you can relate to the best and *always* mark the centre of the flower before you start.

Q11. 'DOES IT MATTER WHICH WAY I WORK A FLOWER?'

I think it does. I insist on all my students working all the flowers by starting the petals at the point at which the stalk joins the flower and working towards the tip of the petal. This means open flowers such as daisies, columbines, etc. are worked out from the centre, and bell shaped flowers are worked down from the top. Tulips are worked up from the bottom.

Always be prepared to turn your work so that you are drawing the ribbon directly towards or away from you, according to the requirements of the stitch being worked, rather than pulling the ribbon sideways and making it difficult to manipulate.

Finally, the centre of the flower is worked last and should overlap the inner edge of the petals so that they appear to go behind the centre, which is the way a flower grows. Working the centre first results in the petals looking as if they are tacked on to the outer edge of the centre and gives a very flat unnatural look.

FLOWERS IN DETAIL

T his chapter contains instructions on how to work each of the flowers used in the designs featured in this book. Many of these flowers are formed by using a combination of stitches that were featured in my earlier publications. All the stitches used are depicted in the glossary at the back of this book.

References are given to the sampler depicted in colour wherever applicable and the symbols used to depict these flowers in the design drawings are shown beside each flower. *The ribbon widths quoted are those used to work the sampler, which is shown in full size in the colour section.*

In the accompanying stitch placement diagrams, bold lines are used to indicate the stitch placement being described, whereas lighter lines and broken lines show previously completed steps.

COLUMBINES

Illustrated in colour on the sampler: 1A to 1C.

Stitches used:
    Ribbon – bullion lazy daisy
               looped straight stitch
    Thread – colonial knots

Colour numbers:
    Ribbon – 4 mm pink 163
              7 mm cream 156

Not recommended for repeated washing.

- Mark a small circle of approximately 2 to 3 mm ($\frac{1}{16}''$ to $\frac{1}{8}''$) in diameter for the centre of the flower. If desired the petal positions can also be marked as shown in the diagram.
Refer to Q10 on page 8 for spacing for five petal flowers.
A chenille needle should be used for all ribbon stitches.

- Using 4 mm ribbon, work five twisted bullion lazy daisy petals (as shown in 1A & B), each being made by taking a stitch about 4 mm ($\frac{3}{16}''$) long and wrapping the ribbon twice around the point of the needle.

- Using 7 mm cream ribbon (No 156), work five looped straight stitch petals around the centre circle. Take care as these stitches are easily disturbed until secured with the centre colonial knots. Use a single strand of DMC thread to work a cluster of colonial knots for the centre, covering the base of the centre petals to hold them firmly in position (1C).

NARCISSUS

Illustrated in colour on the sampler: 1D & E.

Stitches used:
Ribbon – straight stitch
    looped straight stitch
Thread – half colonial knot

Washable when worked in 2 or 4 mm ribbon.

This flower is worked in exactly the same way as the columbine except that the outer petals are worked in straight stitch.

- Mark a small circle for the centre of the flower. Using 4 mm ribbon, work six straight stitch petals around the outer edge of the centre circle.
- Using 4 mm ribbon in apricot, yellow or gold, work four or five looped straight stitches for the trumpet.
- Using a single strand of embroidery thread, fill the centre with half colonial knots, carefully working over the base of the looped stitches to hold them firmly in place.
- Work leaves, using couched twisted ribbon stitch.

BELL SHAPED FLOWERS

Illustrated in colour on the sampler: 2A to 2C.

Stitches used:
Ribbon – bullion lazy daisy
    straight stitch
    ribbon stitch

Washable with care.

Use a large crewel or fine chenille needle and 2 mm ribbon.
 Turn your work upside down so that you start each petal at the point at which the stalk will join the flower.

- Work a single straight stitch as shown in 2A.
- Work a bullion lazy daisy stitch – wrapping the ribbon once around the needle – on each side of the straight stitch to create a tiny fan shape. Pull the stitch firmly and anchor the point of the bullion into an outward curve.
- Work a ribbon stitch over the centre of the bell, covering the first straight stitch completely.
- Hang the bell from the stem with a short straight stitch worked in thread.

TULIPS

Illustrated in colour on the sampler: 2D & E.

Washable.

- Using 4 mm ribbon, depict tulips by working a bell shaped flower the other way up and anchoring the bullion lazy daisy stitches straight, instead of pulling them to one side.

LILAC

Illustrated in colour on the sampler: 4A.

Stitch used:
    Ribbon – colonial knots
Colour numbers:
    Ribbon – 2 mm light & dark mauve 23 & 179 or
            white & cream 1 & 34

Washable.

This flower works best if you use two shades of mauve, or white and cream mixed, to form the flower heads.

- Scatter small knots as shown in the sampler.
- Fill in the spaces, using the second colour. Pack the knots very closely so that the flower head is raised up on the fabric.

BILLY BUTTONS

Illustrated in colour on the sampler: 4B.

Stitch used:
  Ribbon – colonial knots

Colour number:
  Ribbon – 2 mm yellow 15

Washable.

These flowers are formed by working the colonial knots into a very tight circle, causing the centre of the cluster to be raised.

- Work a single knot for the centre.
- Work six or seven knots in a tight circle around the centre knot.
- Work a second circle around the outside of the centre cluster. It is important to pull the knots of this row in towards the centre of the flower by working the needle at an angle, sliding it in and out under the edge of the previous row. This helps to push the centre of the flower up, giving the finished flower a more rounded look.

PAPER DAISIES

Illustrated in colour on the sampler: 3A & B.

Stitches used:
  Ribbon – ribbon stitch, flat and looped
  Thread – colonial knots

Colour numbers:
  Ribbon – 2 mm white 1 or pale pink 157 or
              pale & dark pink 157 & 163

Not recommended for repeated washing.

These little daisies are similar to those detailed in *Silk Ribbon Embroidery for Gifts and Garments*, but this new way of working ribbon stitch gives a more delicate finish to the tips of the raised petals.
  A crewel needle is used throughout.

- Draw a small circle for the flower centre.
- Work the base row of petals, as shown in 3A, using flat ribbon stitch.
- A second row of raised petals is added, working looped ribbon stitch inside the centre circle. Each

petal is formed by first passing the needle through the ribbon at a point that will become the tip of the petal when the stitch is complete (approximately 4 mm ($^3/_{16}$″) from the point where the ribbon emerges from the fabric). Continue pulling the needle through the centre of the ribbon until all the ribbon has passed through the hole. Complete the stitch as for a looped straight stitch, hooking a second needle into the loop as you pull the ribbon through. Control the loop with the second needle until the previously formed point is at the tip of the petal. (See also Stitch Glossary.) Work eight to ten of these shaped petals around the centre circle before anchoring them carefully with a cluster of tiny colonial knots, using a single strand of DMC embroidery thread.

TINY BLOSSOM

Illustrated in colour on the sampler: 3E.

Stitches used:
    Ribbon – straight stitch
    Thread – colonial knots
              straight stitch

Washable.

These tiny four petal flowers are quick to work, make a useful fill-in for larger designs and are very pretty used on miniature pieces, such as jewellery.

- Using 4 mm ribbon, work four petal flowers as shown in 3E.
- Work a cross stitch in fine thread between the petals and finish the centre with a half or full colonial knot. If you work the knot across the threads, as they cross in the flower centre, this will help to keep the knot from disappearing into the centre of the flower if all the petals are radiating from the same centre point.

FANTASY FLOWERS

Illustrated in colour on the sampler: 3C & D.

Stitches used:
    Ribbon – straight stitch
            colonial knots

Washable.

These pretty flowers can be varied in size according to the size of the bead used for the centre. A tiny pearl has been used for the centre of the flower on the sampler.

- Surround the pearl with six or seven colonial knots worked in 2 mm ribbon a shade darker than the outside petals.

- Divide and mark the outer ring into six equal sections as shown in the diagram.

- Using 4 mm ribbon, back stitch two straight stitches, one directly over the top of the other, between each of the sections marked.

STRAIGHT STITCH LEAVES

Illustrated in colour on the sampler: 4C & D.

Stitches used:
    Ribbon – straight stitch
    Thread – stem stitch

Washable.

Straight stitch using 2 mm ribbon works well as a fill-in, as can be seen from the heart shaped leaves I have used in several of the designs featured in this book.

Each stitch is worked so that it just overlaps the preceding stitch. The use of a fine silk thread (Kanagawa Silk Stitch or No 50) or a fine metallic thread, in a fine stem stitch, helps to smooth the outline. Veins may be added and are particularly useful on larger leaves, as they are stitched over the ribbon and help to hold it down firmly.

It is very important to spread the ribbon carefully for this stitch so that the edges do not curl in any way.

- Draw the leaf outline, including the centre vein.

- Using 2 mm green ribbon, work a straight stitch at the tip of the petal as shown in 1C.

- Fill in one side of the leaf, working out from the centre line to the outer edge (4C).
- Starting from the top, fill in the other half of the leaf, again working away from the centre.
- Using fine thread a shade lighter or darker, according to preference, outline the leaf with small stem stitching. Use straight stitch for the veins, couching in place where necessary.

STEM STITCH ROSES

Illustrated in colour on the sampler: 4E.

Stitches used:
  Ribbon – stem stitch
         colonial knots

Not recommended for frequent washing.

This is yet another way to work a rose or camellia. It is quick and easy to do, but not as durable on clothing as the rolled roses that are detailed in *Silk Ribbon Embroidery for Gifts and Garments* and in the next item — One Sided Rolled Rose.
   Two shades of the selected colour of 2 mm ribbon are required.

- Using the darkest shade of ribbon, work four colonial knots in a tight circle.
- Work a row of small stem stitches around these knots, bringing the needle up through the fabric between the knots and the loop of ribbon.
  Tighten the stitches gently, leaving a soft loop for each petal.
- Using the paler ribbon, work a second row of stem stitches around the outside, leaving each in a soft fold.

ONE SIDED ROLLED ROSE

Illustrated in colour on the sampler: 5A & B.

Stitches used:
    Ribbon – single whipped stitch
          straight stitch

Washable.

This rose is another version of the rolled roses introduced in my book *Silk Ribbon Embroidery for Gifts and Garments*. It is featured on the nightgown yoke, but could be used to good effect on anything from baby wear to blouses, collars, etc., as it is very hard wearing.

Two shades of the selected colour of 4 mm ribbon are required.

- Start the rose, using the darker shade of ribbon, with two straight stitches, one directly over the other, for the flower centre. Make these stitches equal in length to the width of the ribbon.

- Work one whipped straight stitch down each side of the centre stitch. 1-2, 3-4 on diagram.

- Place three whipped stitches around the base of the flower, working the centre stitch first, then one stitch on each side (5-6, then 7-8 and 9-10 on the diagram).

- Using the lighter shade of ribbon and commencing at point 1, work five overlapping stitches around base of flower and up to point 3 on the left hand side.

Note that the needle always comes up on the odd numbers and goes down on the even numbers, then comes back through the fabric at the odd number point to start the wrapping process.

  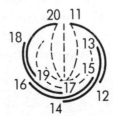

DAISIES

Illustrated in colour on the sampler: 5C.

Stitches used:
   Ribbon – whipped straight stitch in 2 mm ribbon

Washable.

The number of stitches used to form this daisy can be varied considerably. They look beautiful with tightly packed stitches forming a neat circular flower; but fifteen petals of tightly worked ribbon take a considerable amount of time and ribbon to produce. Ten petals were used for each flower on the christening gown and the teddy bear, using method 1 given below.
   The daisies can be worked in two different ways.

Method 1
The petals can be arranged around a marked centre as shown in 3A, leaving room for a bead or a cluster of knots for the centre.

- Work each whipped stitch from the centre out, wrapping the outer end of the stitch a little more than the inner end.

Method 2
For working a daisy as shown in 5C.

- Use a stiletto or large needle to make a hole in the base fabric.
- Working from the *outside* into the centre, lay down a straight stitch, coming up at 1 and going down through the centre hole and back out at 1. Pull the stitch firmly and then wrap it, working in towards the centre and back out to the outer edge. The stitch should be fatter on the outer third. Anchor the stitch by passing the needle to the back of the fabric, gently pulling the stitch into a slight curve.

- Bring the needle up at point 3 and repeat the process.
- Continue working the stitches close to each other in a tight circle. You will need 14 to 16 petals to complete the circle.

KANGAROO PAW

Illustrated in colour on the sampler: 6A to 6C.

Stitches used:
Ribbon – whipped straight stitch
whipped running stitch

Colour numbers:
Ribbon – 2 mm red 49 & green 20.

Washable with care.

This distinctive looking flower is easy to work and looks very realistic.

- The stems are worked in whipped running stitch. Using red 49, 2 mm ribbon, work the ribbon firmly to form a smooth stem.

- Using green 20, 2 mm ribbon, work single whipped straight stitch, as shown in the sampler 6B, for the flower head. The green stitches should touch the red stem at their base.

- Using red 2 mm ribbon, work a back stitch over the base of each green stitch where it joins the stem. Complete with leaves worked in green 20, 2 or 4 mm ribbon, using couched twisted ribbon stitch.

BANKSIA NUTS

Illustrated in colour on the sampler: 5D & E.

Stitches used:
Ribbon – half colonial knots
looped straight stitch
Colour numbers:
Ribbon – 4 mm brown 54

Washable.

Use a fine chenille or medium crewel needle.

- Draw a cone shaped nut and mark small straight lines at random over the area.

- Fill in the nut with half colonial knots, leaving small gaps at each line mark.

- Work two looped straight stitches on each marked line. These should look a little like a slightly open mouth.

- Finish by working one or two half colonial knots between the looped stitches to hold them firmly in place, taking care not to disturb the straight stitches.

BOTTLEBRUSH

Illustrated in colour on the sampler: 7A to 7C.

Stitches used:
Ribbon – colonial knots
whipped running stitch
Thread – looped straight stitch
colonial knots
bullion stitch (optional)

Colour numbers:
Ribbon – 4 mm brown 54 & green 20
2 mm red 49 or 2
DMC stranded thread – brown 3031
Kanagawa 1000 silk thread – brown 54
(for bullion stitch)

Washable with care.

It is not possible to depict a bottlebrush in full flower, but flower heads that are just coming into bloom make an ideal subject.

- Work the branches using whipped running stitch, or long bullion stitches couched into shape. I use fifty to sixty wraps for bullion stitches, however these can be worked in shorter stages as the joins are easily covered with the nut clusters.

- Old nut clusters are formed on the same stems as the new flower heads. Using brown 4 mm ribbon, work clusters of nuts in colonial knots up the bottom half of the branch. Change to green ribbon and repeat with clusters of green colonial knots towards the top of the branch.

- Using a single strand of brown thread and a fine straw needle, work a colonial knot in the centre of each brown ribbon knot.

- Using 2 mm red ribbon and a fine crewel needle, work the ribbon into the centre of the green knots. Work a tiny looped straight stitch into the knots at the tip of the cluster. Towards the bottom of the cluster, take the ribbon down through the knots from the front of the work, leaving a short tail. Back stitch firmly at the back and bring the needle back through to the front, through the same knot. Cut the ribbon and fray the ends with the point of a sharp needle. Trim the ends until they are short and fluffy.

- Add ribbon stitch leaves, making them long and slender.

A circle of rubber (cut from a rubber glove) or a 'grabit' (available from patchwork supply shops) will help reduce stress on the fingers, if used to pull the needle through the knots when working this last step.

GUM TREE

Stitches used:
    Ribbon – Portuguese stem stitch
        ribbon stitch

Colour numbers:
    Ribbon – 2 mm brown 140, tan 77 & green 20
    Madeira gold/black thread No 5014
    (used for outlining)

Not washable.

- Fill in the tree trunk with lines of Portuguese stem stitch, continuing some of the lines on to form the main branches. Add some side branches in thread before working clusters of leaves in ribbon stitch, using green ribbon.

- The Madeira thread is couched along some of the lines of stem stitch as a highlight.

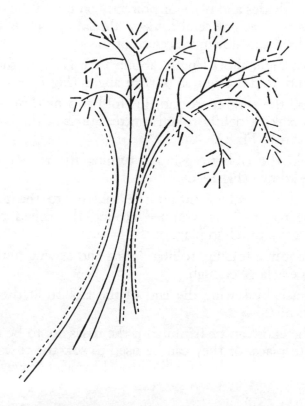

CHAPTER THREE

FOLDED ROSES

Folded roses are very popular as they can be used in many forms of decoration. Worked in silk ribbon, they are very soft and delicate and, because of the fineness of the ribbon, a lovely shaded effect can be achieved by sewing together two ribbons of different colours. 7 mm ribbon is used for the posy brooch, but it is possible to make folded roses from 2 and 4 mm ribbon. The narrower ribbons are ideal for miniature work, but, being so tiny, they do need very nimble fingers.

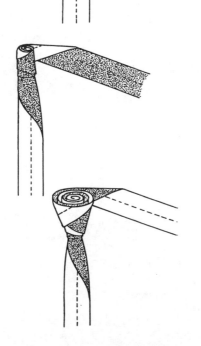

There are many other types of ribbon that are also suitable, so that once the technique is mastered the possibilities are endless.

I prefer to stitch the ribbon at the base of the flower as I work. It is also possible to use glue to stabilise the petals. The same techniques can be used to make the flowers on wired stems. Stick or sew the first fold of the ribbon over a wire stem, after bending the end of the wire over, and proceed as described below.

- Take two pieces of 7 mm silk ribbon in complementary shades and place one directly on top of the other. Using machine embroidery thread in a matching colour, sew down the centre of the strip.

- Holding a short length, about 5 cm (2″), in the left hand, fold the ribbon at right angles (Fig 1).

- Roll the ribbon around this fold two or three times to make a tightly rolled centre. Stitch at the base of this roll (Fig 2).

- Fold the ribbon again by turning the ribbon back and down (Fig 2).

- Continue rolling, *lifting* the fold up to the top of the roll as it is wrapped around the rolled centre (Fig 3). Stitch in place at the base.

- Continue folding, rolling, *lifting* and sewing until the rose is large enough.

- Finish by sewing the end of the ribbon at the base of the flower.

- The ends can be trimmed if the roses are to be glued into place, or they can be used to sew the roses into place as described for the brooch project (page 59).

CHAPTER FOUR

BUTTERFLIES

B utterflies are always popular with embroiderers and they offer such a variety of shape and colour, making the possibilities of design endless.

The butterflies used in the designs shown in this book fall into three categories.

1. Butterflies copied from nature; as used on the clock face and embroidery caddy.

2. Fantasy butterflies; as used for the tray design and on the back cover.

3. Tiny fantasy butterflies; worked on evenweave fabric from charted designs.

All these butterflies are worked using the same basic straight stitch, so that each new stitch worked just overlaps the previous one, thus covering the background fabric completely.

It is very important to pay careful attention to spreading the ribbon for each individual stitch, so that the ribbon lays flat and does not curl at the edges.

Many of these stitches are quite long and their wearability has been increased by working over the top of them using fine silk thread (Kanagawa No 50 is ideal) or fine metallic thread. Machine embroidery thread can also be used for this purpose.

The fine top stitching can be worked in a random design, or in staight lines that run across the direction of the ribbon stitching. The large fantasy butterfly pictured demonstrates the use of both of these methods.

I find the 2 mm ribbon is easier to work than the 4 mm, however the colour range is more limited, so it may sometimes be necessary to use 4 mm ribbon in order to obtain the required colour. This was the case for some of the butterflies copied from nature: the Cairns Birdwing butterfly (12 o'clock on the clock face), for example.

There are two ways of blending from one colour to another. In the large fantasy butterfly, each section was worked with the stitches meeting end to end and the resulting gap in between rows filled with outline stitches worked in ribbon or thread and couched into place. For a more natural blending of colour the stitches can be interleaved, so that the ends of the stitches overlap. This is shown clearly in the overlap between red and black on the Red Lacewing butterfly (6 o'clock on the clock face).

The tiny butterflies are also worked in straight stitch, using evenweave fabric, and, as detailed in the individual project instructions, the designs can be counted out square by square.

Butterflies are also very effective used as an applique design, decorated with a variety of outline stitches and beads, etc., as illustrated on the back cover.

BUTTERFLIES FROM NATURE

Good reproductions can be achieved by copying accurate colour pictures as closely as possible. (Good colour photographs of the first four butterflies detailed here are to be found on page 190 of *Australia's Wilderness Heritage Vol 2 – Flora & Fauna*, published by Weldon Publishing.)

The easiest way to transfer these butterfly pictures is to carefully cut a template, from a tracing or photocopy, and trace the outline directly on to the fabric, using a fine point fadeable marker or water erasable pen.

GENERAL INSTRUCTIONS

All butterflies are worked in long straight stitch, all small stitches such as spots are worked over the top of the base layer. These help to anchor the longer stitches and make the work more secure.

Veins also help to anchor long stitches firmly; make sure they are worked across rather than in line with the base stitching.

The body of the butterfly is divided into sections and, working satin stitch or herringbone stitch using a single strand of embroidery thread, each of the sections is filled in turn.

The feelers are worked with Kanagawa silk thread No 50 or any fine black thread such as machine embroidery thread. Couch a long straight stitch into place and finish with a short back stitch at the top of the feeler.

Cairns Birdwing (Ornithoptera priamus euphorion) ——

Ribbon required:

4 mm	yellow	No 119
	green	No 94
	black	No 4
2 mm	black	No 4

Thread required:
  black (body & feelers)

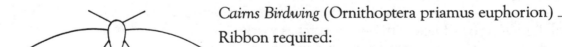

- Trace the outline carefully.
- Using green, work three long stitches along the front edge of the front wings.
- Change to black and continue to fill in with long straight stitches.

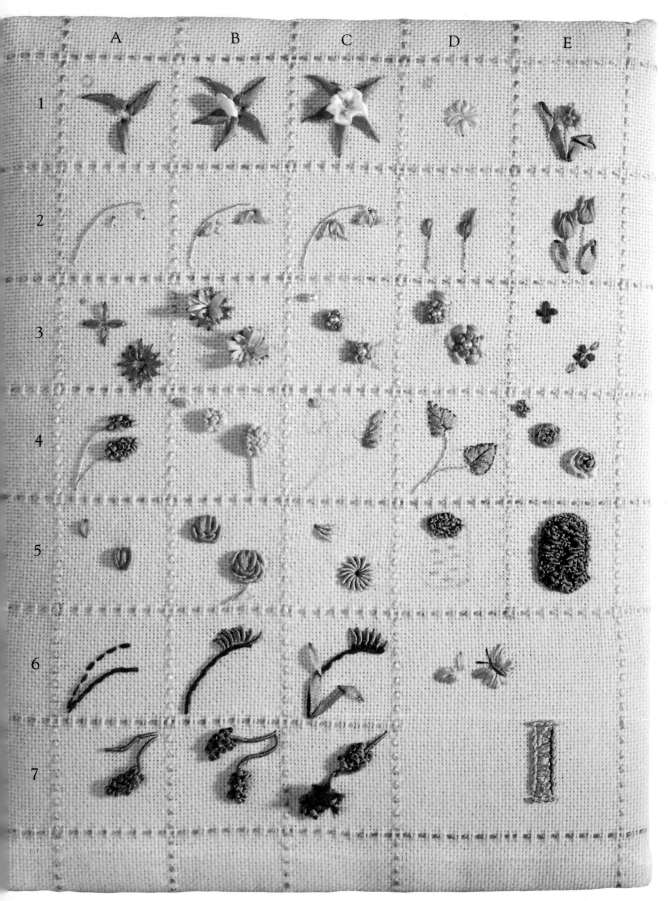

SAMPLER SHOWING DETAILS OF FLOWER CONSTRUCTION

TEDDY BEAR, CHRISTENING GOWN OR PETTICOAT, AND MATINEE JACKET

NIGHTGOWN YOKE AND CUSHION WITH EMBROIDERED HEARTS AND ROSES

EMBROIDERED KNITTED VEST AND JEWELLERY CADDY

CLOCK WITH BUTTERFLIES AND WILDFLOWERS

LARGE FANTASY BUTTERFLY

WIRED POPPIES AND BUTTERFLY

AUSTRALIAN-THEME CRAZY PATCHWORK BAG

BARETTE, BROOCH AND PERFORATED PAPER BOXES

Folded Rose Brooch, Brooch and Card, and Initialed Handkerchief

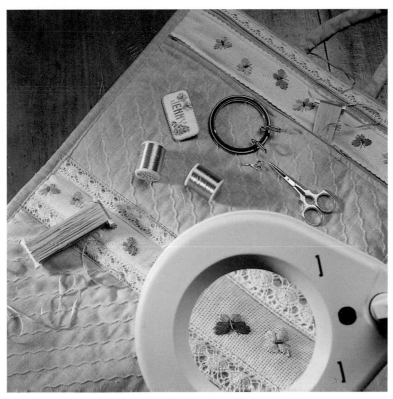

Embroidery Caddy and Luxo Lamp

EMBROIDERY CADDY WITH SAMPLER DESIGN COVER

- With yellow, work over the black, two stitches along the inner edge and three short stitches towards the back edge of each front wing.
- The back wings are worked in yellow, overlaid with a few green stitches and three tiny black dots along the back edge.
- Finish the front edge of the front wings by working a row of whipped running stitches in black along the edge of the green stitches, pulling the stitches tight to form a very thin line.
- Edge the back wings with a row of palastrina stitch, using 2 mm black ribbon.
- Use black embroidery thread to fill in the body area with satin stitch or layered herringbone stitch.
- Work feelers.

Mountain Blue (Papilio ulysses) ———————————

Ribbon required:

2 mm	blue	No 116
	black	No 4
	white	No 1

Thread required:
  brown (body)
  black (feelers & veins)

- Trace the outline and also mark the outline of the blue section.
- Fill in the blue area with long straight stitches.
- Work the outer black area, overlapping the stitches between the ends of the inner blue area.
- Finish the front edge of the front wings with a thin row of whipped running stitch in black.
- Work a black dot in the blue area towards the front of the wing.
- Edge the back wings with palastrina stitch in black. Using white ribbon, work a tiny looped straight stitch in each indentation along the outer edge.
- Fill in the body with satin stitch in brown thread.
- Work veins and feelers in black.

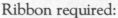

Lacewing (Cethosia cydippe) ——————————————

Ribbon required:

2 mm	blue	No 45
	pink	No 157 & 112
	brown	No 140
	white	No 1

Thread required:
    gold (body)
    black (feelers)

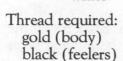

- Trace the outline carefully and mark the outline for the pink section.
- Fill in the inner wing area with pale pink.
- Work the outer area in blue, making the stitches meet but not overlap.
- Add white patches through the blue area.
- Work tiny spots of deep pink in the blue area of the back wings. Outline the pale pink wing sections with tiny straight stitches in the darker pink, working across from the pink to the blue stitching.
- Finish the front edge with a row of thin whipped running stitch in brown.
- Edge the remainder of the wings with palastrina stitch, working looped straight stitches in white along the outer edge in each indentation. Further looped stitches are added inside the brown edging at the back of the wings.
- Fill in the body with satin stitch in gold embroidery thread.
- Work feelers.

Red Lacewing (Cethosia cydippe chrysippe) —————————

Ribbon required:

2 mm	red	No 48
	black	No 4
	white	No 1

Thread required:
    black (body & feelers)

- Trace the outline and also mark the outline for the red section.

- Fill in the inner wing sections with red ribbon.
- Work the outer wing sections in black, overlapping the two sections.
- Work the white flashes over the black stitching.
- Finish the front edge of the front wing with whipped running stitch and edge the remainder of the wings with palastrina stitch.
- Fill in the body with black.
- Work feelers in black.

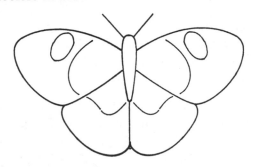

Lesser Wanderer (Danaus chrysippus) _____

Ribbon required:

4 mm	black	No 4
	white	No 1
	gold	No 54
	tan	No 107
2 mm	black	No 4

Thread required:
  brown (body)
  black (feelers)

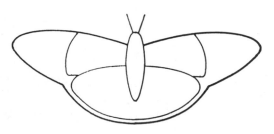

- Trace the outline.
- Work the inner front wing section in tan.
- Fill in the back wing with gold.
- Fill in the outer edge of the front wing in black and overstitch the white flashes.
- Work the front edge with fine whipped running stitch in 2 mm black ribbon and edge the remainder of the wings with palastrina stitch.
- Work looped straight stitch in white along the outer edge of the palastrina stitch.
- Work the body in brown and the feelers in black.

FANTASY BUTTERFLIES

Fantasy Butterfly I ————————————————

For the original design shown:
Ribbon required:

2 mm	gold	No 54
	sand	No 34
	green	No 63
	brown	No 140

Thread required:
Kanagawa metallic copper No 402
Candlelight metallic copper
stranded mid brown (body & feelers)

- Transfer the design to the fabric, marking the dividing lines as well as the outline.

- Fill in each area with straight stitch, working across the panels in the direction of the arrows. The stitches of each panel should meet end on.

- Using the fine metallic thread, back stitch along each of the three front wing sections and around the 'eye' area. This 'eye' section is filled in with rows of whipped running stitch and colonial knots.

- Work random straight stitching over the green section of the back wings using the fine metallic thread.

- Couch around the green areas with 'Candlelight', held down with the fine metallic thread.

- Outline the remainder of all the sections with Portuguese stem stitch in brown.

- Work the body in layered herringbone stitch, using three strands of embroidery cotton.

- Feelers are worked in Portuguese stem stitch with a single strand of thread.

Fantasy Butterfly II —————————————————

(Pictured on the back cover.)

These butterflies are appliqued using a shaded fabric for the applique and then embellished with embroidery.

- Applique the design. See page 37.

- The front wings are outlined with two rows of whipped running stitch, one worked on the edge of the applique fabric, the other on the base fabric as close to the edge of the applique as possible.

- The back wings are worked with a single row of palastrina stitch or Portuguese stem stitch.

- Crystal beads are added for extra sparkle.

- Bodies are worked in satin stitch and the feelers couched into place.

CHARTED DESIGN BUTTERFLIES

The charts show the stitching pattern for these little butterflies. They can be varied in size according to the evenweave fabric used.

- Start each design at the front of the front wing and work both front wing sections before working the back wing sections.
- The body can be worked with a single wrapped straight stitch in brown ribbon or a bullion stitch worked in Kanagawa 1000 No 52 or 54.
- Feelers are worked in fine black thread, using a long straight stitch with a short back stitch at the tip.

The butterflies shown on the inside of the sewing caddy are worked in variegated silk ribbon hand-dyed by Mary Hart-Davies of Somers, Victoria.

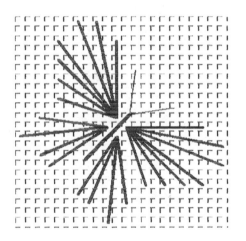
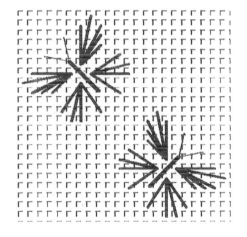

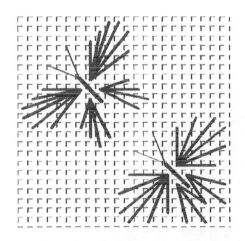
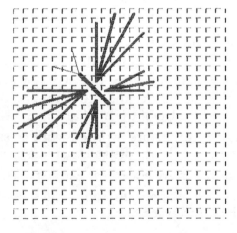

CHAPTER FIVE

RUCHING RIBBON

T his has been used on the patchwork bag for the initial and the opal cluster. It can also be used for outlining a design or making flowers.

- Using a fine straw or crewel needle and fine silk thread, run a gathering thread of tiny stitches in zigzag pattern through a length of 4 or 7 mm ribbon.

- Pull up gently until the ribbon is nicely gathered.
- Arrange and tack into place before ending off the gathering thread, so that you can adjust the amount of ribbon required for your design.

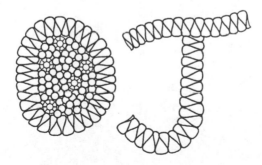

The opal cluster has been formed with ruched ribbon surrounding colonial knots and diamantes and the initial by ruched ribbon on its own.

CHAPTER SIX

INITIALS

The use of lettering or initials can add a personal touch to your embroidery, with many sources of design for cross stitch lettering available that can be combined with silk ribbon work.

The alphabet included in this book offers the possibility of working letters in applique and then using ribbon work for further decoration, in a similar way to that described for the butterflies.

Letters can be filled in with straight stitch and overstitched with highlight thread, as used on the butterflies and illustrated on the bottom right hand corner of the embroidery caddy. These initials were worked in ribbon hand-dyed by Mary Hart-Davies.

Another use would be to outline the shape of the letter with one of the outline stitches and then fill the shape with flowers or an abstract design.

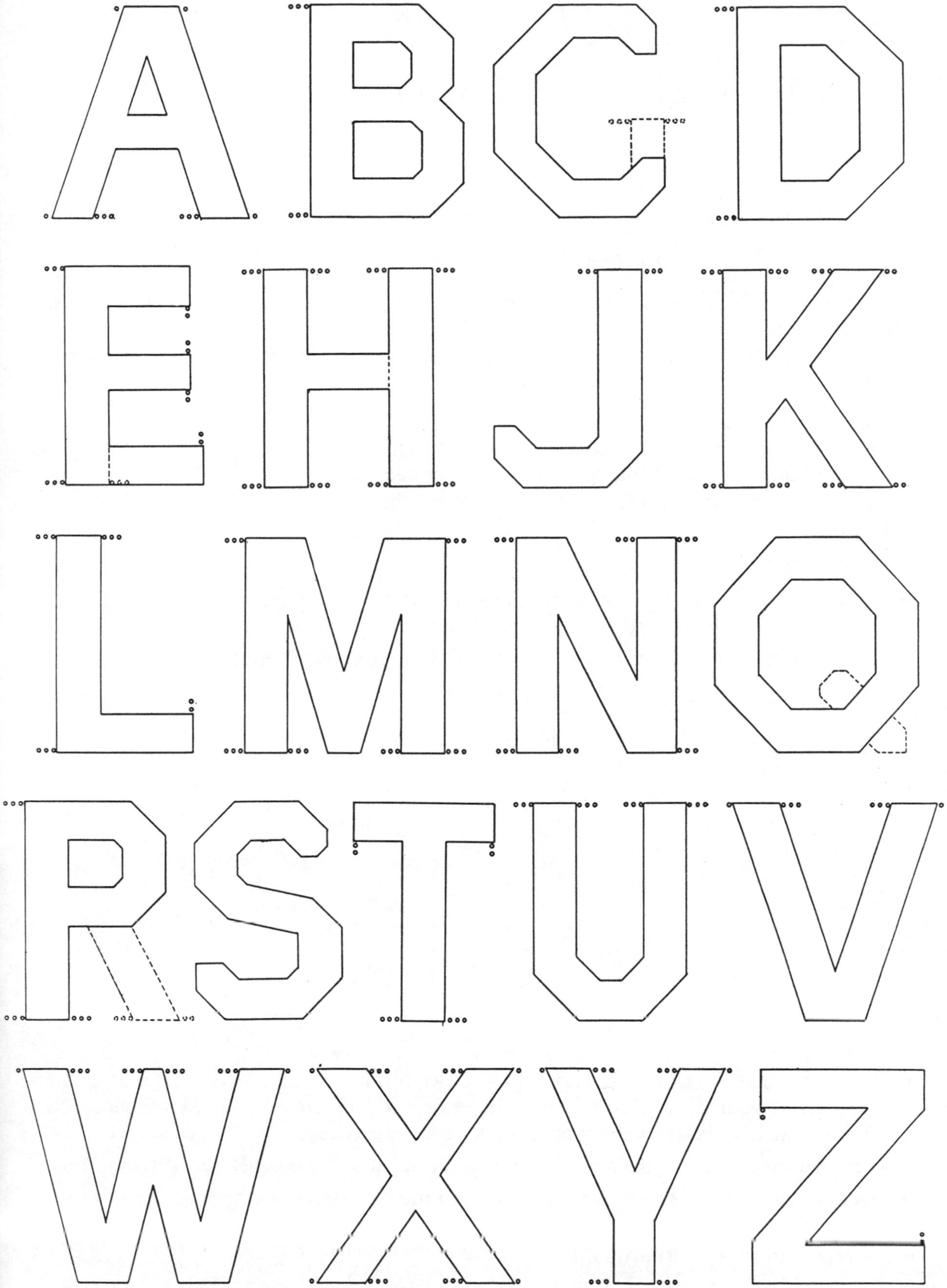

A B C D

E H J K

L M N O

R S T U V

W X Y Z

CHAPTER SEVEN

WIRED FLOWERS AND BUTTERFLIES

LARGE WIRED FLOWERS/POPPIES

These flowers are easy to make and very effective in floral arrangements, for decorating hats and as hair pieces.

The size is easy to adjust for individual requirements. General instructions follow.

Requirements:
Silk organza in desired colours
Fine cotton-covered cake decorating or florist wire
Stamens and/or back shank buttons for flower centres
Silk ribbon to match or blend with the chosen fabric
Felt or suede to cover the back of the flower centre
Fabric glue

- For each flower cut two pieces of fabric 14 cm (5½″) wide x 40 cm (16″) long. Fold in half lengthwise and press firmly to crease along the long edge.

- Place a piece of wire between the two layers along the folded edge.

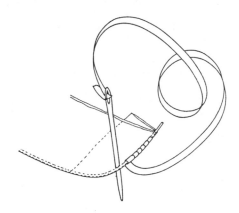

- Curve the wire at each end and fold the double fabric to the back, pinning the wire firmly against this fold. Whip the entire edge with ribbon. Make sure you stitch through all layers when working over the curved edge.

- Trim the excess fabric from folded ends, cutting it away against the stitching line.

- Overlap the curved edges slightly before running a strong gathering thread along the lower edge.

- Make a second layer to match.

- Thread a length of wire through the button shank. Cover the button by cutting a circle of fabric, run a gathering thread around the outside edge and pull tightly over the button. Tie the gathering thread off firmly.
- Stick or sew stamens around the button if required.
- Thread the wire through the centre of the wired petals. Pull up the gathers and tie off firmly. Use the ends of these threads in a needle to sew firmly in place.
- Add the second layer behind the first, making sure the overlapped ends of the strip are opposite those on the first layer.
- Glue a circle of felt to the back of the flower to cover the gathers.
- Shape the flower petals by moulding the wired edges over your fingers.

Flowers of this size are used in the floral arrangement and on the sun hat.

Smaller flowers made from strips of fabric 7 cm x 35 cm (3" x 14") make lovely hair ornaments, button-holes or can be used to decorate an evening bag.

Extra sparkle can be added by using gold or diamante buttons for the centres, tiny beads for stamens and pearl sprays in place of leaves.

WIRED BUTTERFLIES

The addition of wire to the wings of the butterflies makes them pliable, so that they can be bent into shapes. They can be used as a brooch, hair slide or as additional decoration in a floral arrangement or picture.

Requirements:
    Silk organza or georgette in desired colours
    Fine cotton-covered cake decorating or florist wire
    2 or 4 mm silk ribbon to match the fabric
    Machine embroidery thread to match the fabric
    Black or brown shaped chenille pipe cleaner for the body
    The sewing machine presser foot with a groove or hole designed to guide a cording thread should also be fitted

- Mark the outline of each pair of wings on to a single layer of fabric and embroider the highlight markings with 2 mm silk ribbon.

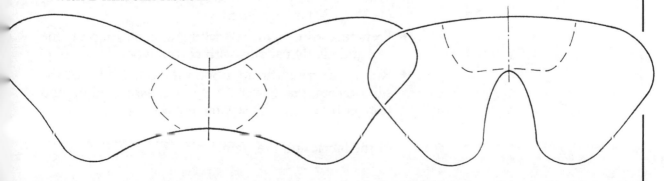

- Set the machine with matching embroidery thread, the appropriate presser foot and a close narrow zigzag stitch.
- Back the embroidered wings with a second layer of fabric and back both layers with a sheet of paper. Thread the thin wire through the hole or groove in the presser foot and, working over the wire, stitch through the fabric and the paper around the outline of each pair of wings.
- Cut out the wings, leaving a 3 mm (⅛″) turning.
- Carefully tear away the paper.
- Using silk ribbon, cover the edges of each wing with overlapping whipped stitches.
- Overlap the wings and tack together.
- Cut a section of the pipe cleaner for the body, fold over the head end neatly and stick or sew in place.

SMALL WIRED FLOWERS/DAISIES

These daisies are worked on a double layer of silk organza, which is trimmed to a small circle after the embroidery is completed.

Requirements:
    Green silk organza (brown or grey can be substituted)
    Wire stems
    Florist tape
    2 mm silk ribbon in flower colours
    Stranded thread for flower centres

For each daisy:
- Mark a small centre on the fabric.
- Work two rows of looped ribbon stitch, as detailed on page 72, around the centre.
- Complete the centre of the flower with colonial knots in fine thread, making sure these knots overlap the ends of the petals to hold them firmly in place.
- Trim the fabric to a circle approximately 4 to 5 cm (1½″ to 2″) in diameter.
- Prepare a wire stem by making a small loop at one end and lightly padding with cotton wool.
- Run a gathering thread around the outer edge of the silk organza, place over the padded wire, pull up and fasten off securely by sewing in place.
- Finish by wrapping with florist tape to cover the ends of the fabric and the stem.

CHAPTER EIGHT

USEFUL BASIC TECHNIQUES

TRANSFERRING A DESIGN TO THE FABRIC

T his can be done in various ways, depending on the type of design you are working with. In most cases, transferring the main design lines, together with the position of the largest flowers, should be enough. Once these have been established, the remainder of the design should be easy to position by eye.

- The main lines can be traced off on to the fabric with a marker pen or pencil, if the design can be seen through the fabric. Try placing the fabric over the design print or tracing, and taping it on to a window, so that the light shines through. This makes an excellent substitute for a light box. (This method can be used to reverse a design; simply tape the design face against the window and trace the design on the back of the paper.)

If the background fabric is too dark to use that method, or if you do not want to mark the project fabric, outlining by machine is an excellent alternative. This method is best where the marking of symmetrical shapes, such as ovals, hearts etc. is required.

- Trace or photocopy the pattern on to a sheet of paper; reverse the design if it is asymmetrical.

- Position and pin the design to the back of the work, placing any backing fabric required between the base fabric and the paper.

- Using a fine thread that matches the surface fabric, sew directly over the design lines you wish to mark. Use a short length stitch when marking tight curves.

The advantage of stitching through the paper is that it prevents any stretch in the fabric as you work, so there is no distortion of the shapes as they are stitched. The fabric can be manipulated and turned smoothly and evenly around curves by gently rotating it; the paper will prevent any uneven stretch or pull.

Once marking is complete, the paper is torn away and the design is ready for embroidery.

APPLIQUE

I find this method — based on working from the back of the design — very easy, and ideal for use with embroidery, as it does not require the use of any adhesive bonding (which can adversely affect the ribbon).

- Prepare a copy of the design on a sheet of paper, reversing the design if necessary. (See 'Transferring a Design to the Fabric'.)

- Position the design on the back of the work.

- Position and pin the applique fabric over the design area on the front of the work.

- Using a short length straight stitch and a bobbin thread to match the applique fabric, stitch around the outline from the back of the work.
- Carefully trim the applique fabric back to the machine line, using small, very sharp, embroidery scissors.
- From the front of the work, zigzag over the edge of the design, working across the straight stitching with a zigzag setting of medium width and length.
- Tear away the paper backing and cover the edging with any one of the outline stitches.

The advantages of working this way are noted in 'Transferring a Design to the Fabric'. Further information on this method of applique can be found in *Silk Ribbon Embroidery 2 — Transform Your Clothes*.

ROLLING AND WHIPPING

This is an excellent way of finishing edges for attaching lace or entredeux. Although originally worked by hand, this process can be quickly completed on any sewing machine that will do a simple zigzag stitch.

To work successfully, fine pure cotton fabrics should be used, the edges must be cut and not torn and a fine sewing thread (No 60 cotton) will produce the best results. No 60 cotton can be obtained from specialist shops that handle heirloom and fine sewing supplies.

Use a stitch length just short of the satin stitch setting and a width setting of $1\frac{1}{2}$ to 2. (The needle should catch about 2 mm ($\frac{1}{16}''$) of the fabric and clear the raw edge as it swings from side to side.) Tighten the top thread tension and work with the fabric wrong side up.

As you stitch along the edge, the fabric should roll over to form a very fine hem. Practice adjusting your machine settings until this works smoothly and neatly.

Working from the right side, place the lace or entredeux edge to edge with the rolled hem and zigzag together, using the finest zigzag setting practicable.

BIAS OR STRAIGHT BINDING

When using lightweight fabrics, cut twice the required width and use the binding folded double.

Match the cut edges, press and sew in place, matching all raw edges. Turn and hem along the fold.

This method is neater, easier to sew and the double thickness gives a smooth finish and reinforces the edge where the most wear occurs.

Be sure to calculate the width required carefully , as there is no adjustment once the band is stitched in place.

MACHINE QUILTING

A small attachment known as a quilting guide is available and often supplied with many brands of sewing machine. This guide is essential for quilting and makes the process very quick and easy to do.

An attractive variation to plain quilting is to use a twin needle and one of the fancy line stitches that many machines have. The use of machine embroidery thread will add an extra sheen to the stitching.

I always work on the diagonal, making the first row across the bottom right hand corner.

Never tack the fabrics together as you need to be able to smooth the top fabric as you go, to prevent small wrinkles. If necessary, pin the fabric and remove the pins as you come to them.

Use a firm batting which will hold its shape and not catch on the feed teeth of the machine. Soft fluffy batting used for hand quilting is not suitable.

Always quilt a piece slightly larger than the size required and cut your pattern out afterwards. This will give a neat edge and any slight distortion that might occur in quilting will not be transferred to your project.

- Cut a piece of fabric and a piece of batting.
- Pin the pieces together, moving across the fabric from the bottom right hand corner to the top left hand corner.
- Set up the machine according to the manufacturer's instructions. Work a small test piece to check tension and spacing.
- Stitch across the bottom right hand corner, starting and finishing 2 to 2.5 cm (1″) from the corner.
- Line the stitched row up with the bar on the quilting guide and stitch a second row.
- Repeat across the fabric, removing the pins and smoothing the surface as you stitch.

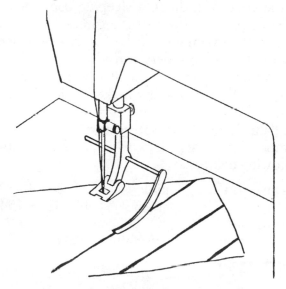

CHAPTER NINE

PROJECTS

CLOTHING

Many ideas for using ribbon embroidery are shown in the colour pages. These are intended to inspire the reader with ideas for using the embroidery on a variety of wearable items.

When choosing a purchased garment or pattern to make your own, bear in mind the following:

- The design should be simple, in order to focus on the embroidery. Other embellishments such as tucks or lace should complement the embroidery but not overshadow it by being too prominent.
- Careful placement of the design so that it does not conflict with darts, etc. that will be sewn later.
- Careful placement of the embroidery to focus attention on the wearer's good figure points, rather than attracting attention to the bad points.
- Embroidery usually looks better on a plain coloured background, however it can be used effectively to highlight and accentuate parts of a background design.
- Finally, give careful consideration to laundering, see page 3, when choosing the fabric for your project.

Matinee Jacket _____

This little jacket, made from wool chalis, is cut from a purchased layette pattern. The same idea could be used on the yoke of a dress, a sleeping bag, cot cover or the bib of a pinafore dress or dungarees.

The decorative quilting is worked with a twin needle and shiny machine embroidery thread.

A fine pellon or one of the lightweight waddings designed especially for clothing makes an ideal backing for quilting. If you do not want such a thick padding, a layer of flannelette is quite satisfactory.

The embroidery design is worked in 2 mm ribbon in the following colours:

Daisies and bow	pink	No 8
Leaves	green	No 31 or 154
Daisies and tiny four petal flowers	off-white	No 1
Forget-me-nots	blue	No 98 or 126

Also used is DMC stranded cotton:

Stems	green
Stamens	pink

- Quilt the fabric and cut out the pattern pieces before working the embroidery.
- Lightly trace the main lines of the design on to the fabric by placing a copy of the design between the quilt batting and the design area.
- Neaten the edges of the cut pieces with a machine zigzag stitch to prevent fraying.
- Work the embroidery:
    - Couch the stems into place, laying two strands of thread with a single strand of matching thread.
    - Work the bow using whipped running stitch.
    - Work the tiny four petal flowers (page 14).
    - Add whipped straight stitch daisies together with tiny clusters of blue colonial knots.
    - Finish the embroidery by adding straight stitch leaves along the stems.
- Finish the garment according to the pattern you are using.

This design is also ideal for collars or cuffs and could be used on the jewellery holder.

Christening Gown or Petticoat Panel _____

This is a very simple design, shown on the hem of a christening gown, but is equally suitable for use around the bottom of a lady's petticoat or across the yoke of a nightgown or blouse.

The christening gown was made from silk batiste, using a smocked bishop day gown pattern *(Simply Smocking S.S.3, by Jenny Bradford)*, lengthened by the addition of lace bands and the embroidered panel.

The design is worked in a lovely cream silk thread 'Kanagawa 380' No 97 and white silk ribbon No 1. The embroidery area is backed with a panel of white silk organza. (See page 4.)

The flowers are whipped straight stitch daisies (page 18) with a tiny pearl at the centre of each one. Feather stitching in cream thread completes the design.

Lady's Nightgown ————————————————————————

The design used here on a lady's nightgown would make a pretty yoke for a blouse or a lovely detachable collar. The same idea can be used as a panel insertion down the front of a blouse.

A decorative strip of fabric can be made, using your own selection of flowers, as an insertion for almost any heirloom sewing design. There are many publications available on heirloom sewing, both by hand and machine, and your local sewing machine specialist should be able to assist you with setting up your machine for this beautiful specialised form of needlework.

To construct a panel:

- Cut a pattern of the garment section to be decorated, from calico or vilene. In the case of the nightgown, it is the front yoke sections.

- Calculate and measure the width of the various strips carefully, taking into consideration the neckline and armhole edge. It is a waste of time to embroider a beautiful rose only to find it comes directly in line with a seam line and will be lost into the seam on construction.

It is more satisfactory and easier to get a neat finish if the fabric is smooth and flat over the seam lines, particularly where any shaping is involved.

- The strips are each rolled and whipped (see page 38), then pieced together using strips of entredeux to form a single piece of fabric from which to cut the correctly sized pattern piece.

  - The nightgown yoke is made up of 3.5 cm (1¼″) wide panels embroidered with roses, alternated with 4 cm (1½″) wide tucked panels, all joined with a fancy entredeux. The embroidered panels are cut 8 cm (3″) wide and embroidered along the centre line, then folded right sides together.

  - Sew into a tube with 5 mm (¼″) turnings.

  - Press the seam open, turn right side out and centre the seam at the back of the panel.

  - Press carefully and attach the entredeux along the folded edge.

This method leaves a neat finish by covering the back of the embroidery but retaining the open look created by the entredeux, which tends to be spoilt if the whole yoke is lined.

Knitted Vest

The flowers used in this design are of an abstract design and the size will depend largely on the size of the beads used for the centre of each flower.

The original design shown is worked in 4 mm ribbon in the following colours:

grey	No 58
pink	No 8 & 157
green	No 154

Also used:
42 seed pearls 3 mm ($\frac{1}{8}$″)
silk organza as required

- Start by cutting a facing of silk organza to fit the neckline of the vest and of 5 cm (2″) width.

    – Neaten the edges of this facing by rolling and whipping or overlocking.

- Carefully trace the design from the pattern on to the silk organza facing, then tack the facing in place inside the neckline of the garment.

- Transfer the main design lines to the front of the work by means of a tacking thread, and working with small stitches from the reverse side.

- I found it sufficient to transfer the lines only, as the flower centres can be pinpointed from the back with the centre bead.

- Work the curved lines using Portuguese stem stitch.

- Complete the remainder of the design with fantasy flowers (page 15), straight edge stitch leaves and the pearls.

- Slip stitch one edge of the facing to the neckline ribbing. Other edge should not need sewing down.

Design on Knitted Vest
Inset: how to adapt for
a round necked garment

TEDDY BEAR

This teddy bear pattern has been included in response to numerous requests for a cuddly bear suitable for a child, as distinct from the heirloom bear featured in my book *Bullion Stitch Embroidery*.

The bear is made from pure wool blanketing and is fully washable. The features are embroidered and the limbs are moveable. Instructions are given for attaching the limbs with buttons, however the pattern is equally suitable for the use of commercial joints if desired.

Materials required:
Woollen blanketing
Fibre-fill stuffing
4 good quality 2-hole buttons
Brown wool for embroidering features
   – tapestry wool or 2 strands of
      Appletons' crewel wool
Extra long doll-making needle
Very strong thread
   – Cotton Pearle No 3 or 5 are ideal
Ribbon for neck bow

- Copy all pattern pieces on to paper, making right and left hand pieces as required. Do not cut out the pattern pieces.
- Position the foot pad, inner arm and left front body pattern pieces on the fabric and sew through the paper around the *cutting* line.
  Stitching the outline of each pattern piece through the paper pattern before cutting out prevents the pieces from stretching and distorting as the bear is constructed.
- Tear away the paper and work the embroidery, before carefully cutting these pieces out just outside the machine stitching.
- Place the inner arm pieces right side down on to a piece of the fabric. Stitch around the *seam* line, through the double thickness, leaving open where marked on the pattern for turning and stuffing.
- Cut the second layer of fabric to match the cutting line of the embroidered inner arm section.
- Position the leg and ear pattern pieces on to *double* fabric. Sew around the *seam* line through all thicknesses, leaving the opening for stuffing and turning where marked.
- Cut along the cutting line after tearing away the paper.
- Tack the foot pads in place, right sides together, and stitch carefully.
- Stitch all the remaining head and body pieces on to a single layer of fabric, sewing around the cutting edge, and mark darts with machine stitching at the same time.
- Remove paper pattern and cut out carefully.
- Stitch all the darts in the side head panels.
- Place side head pieces right sides together and sew seam A-B.
- Match head gusset points C-A-C to side head sections C-A-C, tack into place and machine stitch carefully, using a small stitch.

- Stitch centre front body seam.
- Stitch centre back body seam, leaving open where the extra seam allowance is shown for turning and stuffing.
- Stitch front body to back body at side seams, matching the centre front and centre back seams at the base.
- Turn all the pieces right side out.
- Stuff head firmly.
- If using commercial joints for the limbs, insert and fix before stuffing the body and limbs firmly.
  Successful stuffing is an art and if done well gives the work a professional finish. Always use a good quality stuffing.
  - Pack small pieces down with a blunt tool such as the handle of a crochet hook or a screwdriver. Gently mould and shape each piece as you work it, keeping it as symmetrical and smooth as possible. Compare the size of matching parts (legs and arms) carefully to ensure that they match in size and shape.

- Close all the openings securely, using ladder stitch.
- Work the eyes, using brown wool. A rose, as worked for wool embroidery, makes an excellent shape.
- Work the nose in satin stitch and add straight stitch lines for the mouth.
- Embroider the flower design around the ear area.
- Ladder stitch the ears in place.
- Using strong thread, sew the head of the bear to the body very firmly, working in ladder stitch around the neck area at least twice.
- To attach the limbs with buttons, proceed as follows:
  - If the long needle will not fit through the button holes, take a long double strand of strong thread and thread through the button, then thread the needle with one end of the double thread. Pass it through the limb and the body of the bear to the other side. Repeat with the other end of the thread. Leave threads untied while repeating the process to attach the other limbs.
  - Pull the threads very firmly and tie off securely, each limb being tied off on the opposite side of the body so that the knot is positioned between the body and the opposite limb.
- Tie a ribbon bow around the neck.

Teddy's eyes

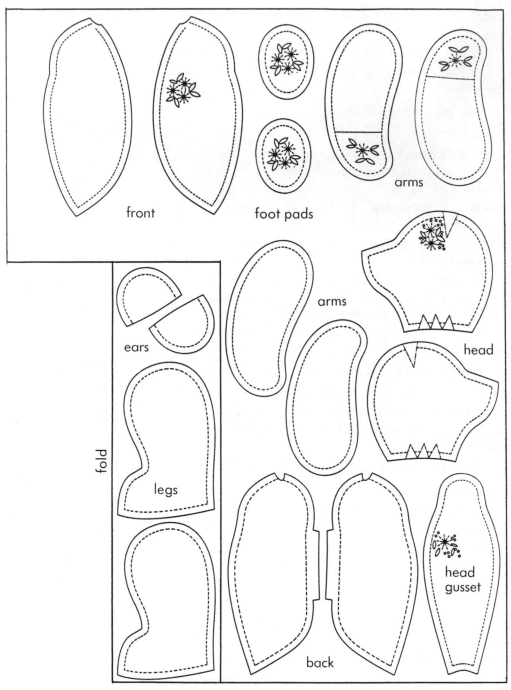

front

foot pads

arms

arms

head

ears

legs

fold

back

head
gusset

quarter scale layout for cutting from
53 cm x 70 cm (21″ x 27½″) material

Teddy Bear

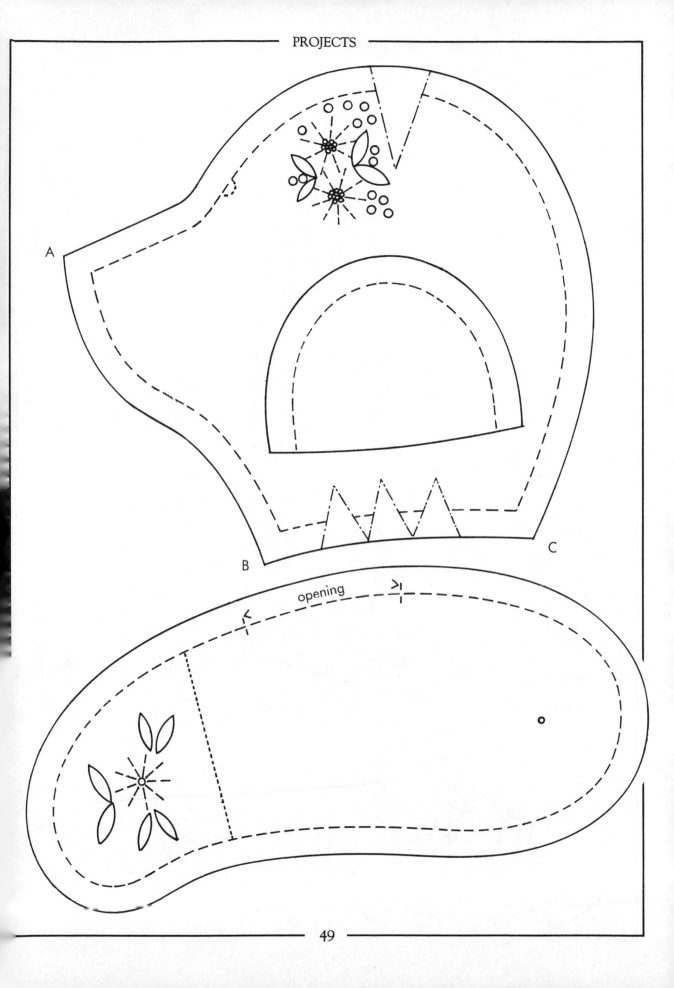

A

B

C

opening

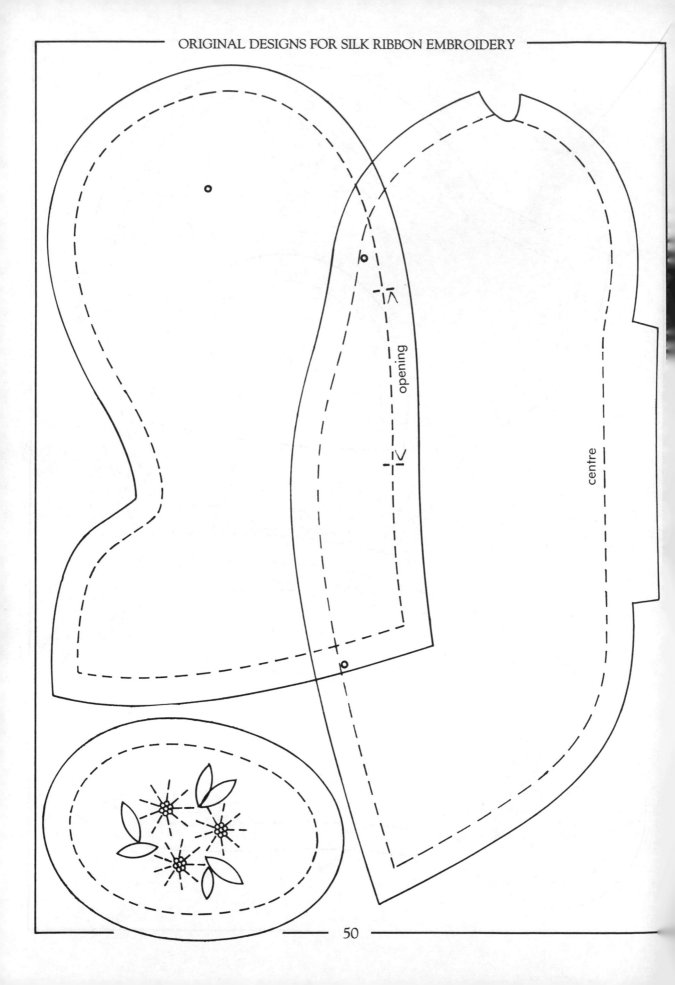

opening

centre

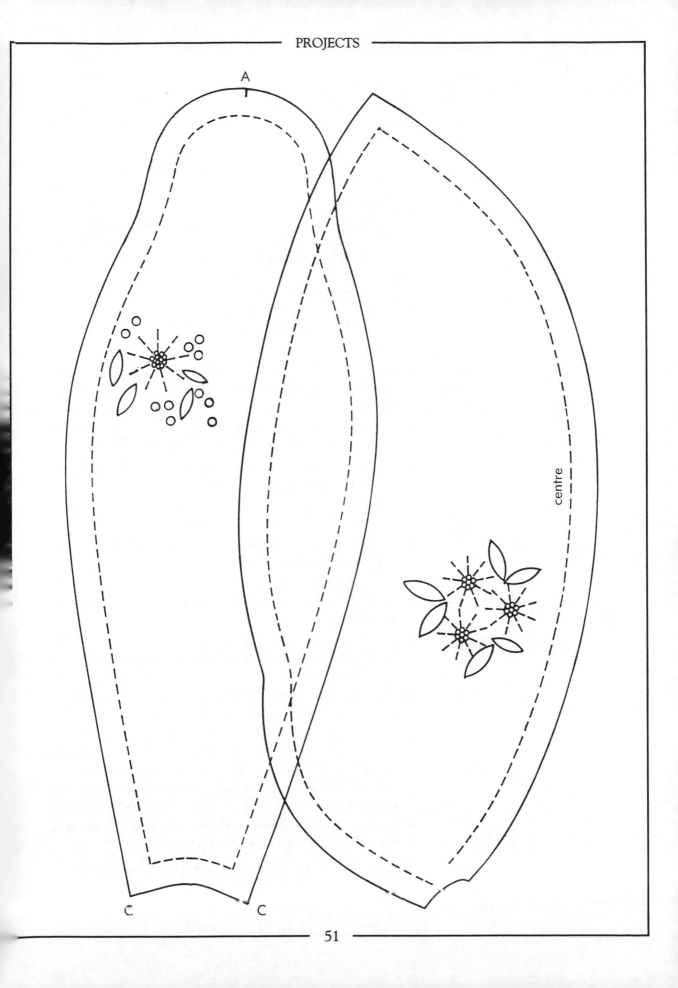

A

centre

C   C

CLOCK

Many people have admired the clock kit that was first featured in *Bullion Stitch Embroidery* and have asked for another design for the embroidery.

This design is also Australian based, depicting four of our beautiful butterflies and some of the new wildflowers featured in this book. However, it is very different and I hope it will appeal to many readers.

A clock kit, including a hand-turned Australian timber surround by my husband Don, is available to order. Details for wood workers are also included on page 53.

This design would also be very effective as a cushion panel, a framed picture or a padded box top.

The background fabric is noil silk used with a backing of pellon fleece.

- Mark the outside and inside edges of the disc and the main design lines from each floral spray as detailed on page 37.
- Work the embroidery, following the details given for the flowers (Chapter 2) and butterflies (Chapter 4).
- Trim the outer fabric to leave a 4 to 5 cm (2") turning *outside* the machine stitch guide line.
- Cut away the centre circle, leaving a similar turning allowance *inside* the inner marked circle.
- Strengthen both these edges on the machine using a close zigzag stitch.
- Cover the hardboard or plywood template with a thin layer of wadding, cutting it flush with the edges of the disc.
- Run a strong thread around the outer edge of the fabric circle and pull to the back, centring over the disc. Tie firmly.
- Clip the inner turnings evenly around the circle to the machine stitched circle.
- Using strong thread, lace the embroidery firmly in place, working across the back of the disc from the outer edge to the inner edge. Make sure the embroidery is correctly orientated in relation to the attaching screws or bolts and the 12 o'clock position.
- Protect with a fabric protector spray, if desired, before bolting into position on the clock.

Mounting this way ensures that the fabric could be removed for dry cleaning if necessary.

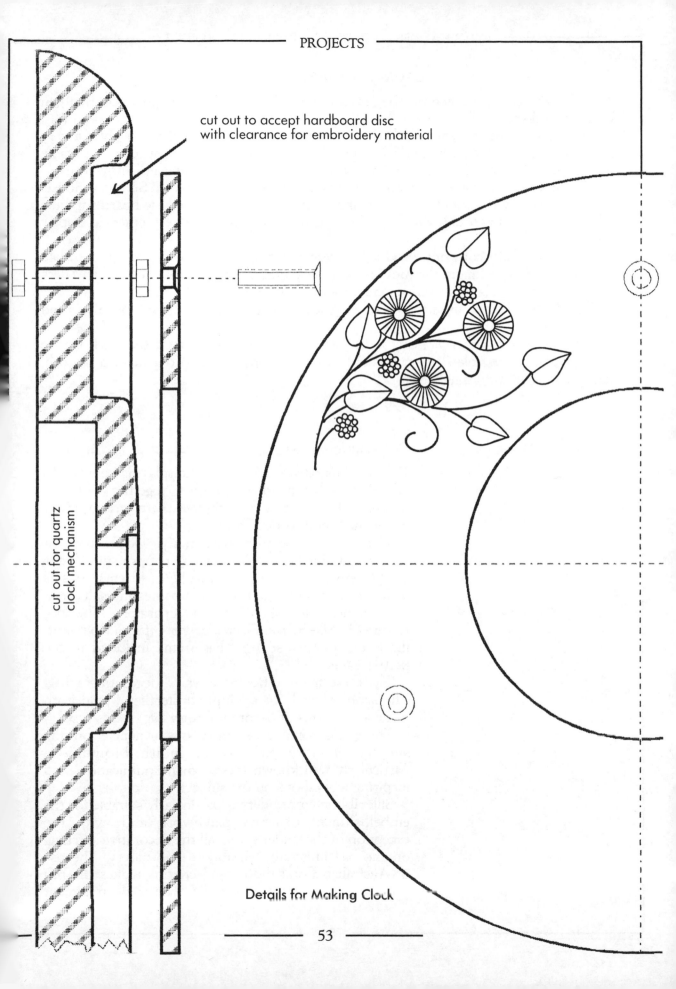

cut out to accept hardboard disc
with clearance for embroidery material

cut out for quartz
clock mechanism

Details for Making Clock

USING COMMERCIAL ITEMS

There is an ever increasing number of commercially manufactured products that can be used to display embroidery.

Choosing to mount your work this way does increase the cost, but it gives a very practical and useful application to the work. Many of these items are particularly suitable for special occasion gifts such as 21st birthday, engagement, wedding and anniversary.

The large butterfly was designed to complement a wooden tray from Sudbury House. The work is easy to mount, by means of stapling or sticking to the base board supplied with the tray. Being totally protected by a glass cover, it makes a very practical display piece.

The Framecraft company produce a wide range of products, including porcelain and crystal pots, miniature frames and jewellery pieces. Their latest range of jewellery mounts are particularly attractive, and are easy to assemble.

The designs I have used for these are shown on page 57, and have been worked on hardanger 22 fabric.

It is important when working small pieces such as this to keep the back of the work as flat as possible (keep twists out of the ribbon) in order to achieve a smooth, flat finish when mounting the work.

Crazy Patchwork Bag _____

This bag illustrates another way of displaying your work. A full range of handbag patterns, together with the necessary frame parts to complete them, are available under the brand name 'Ghees'.

This bag is made from pattern style 3801, using an 8″ Straight Hex Frame. A multi-size pattern suitable for 8″ (20 cm), 10″ (25 cm) and 17″ (43 cm) bags is included, but only one size frame comes in each pack. The frames can be purchased separately. The bag featured in *Silk Ribbon Embroidery for Gifts and Garments* illustrates another style of bag frame included in the pattern range.

There are many different ways of decorating a bag. The large butterfly or applique butterflies would both make ideal forms of decoration for a bag of this type.

There are some excellent books available on the subject of crazy patchwork. Judith Montana is particularly well known for her many publications and inspiring workshops on the subject.

Silk ribbon embroidery is particularly suitable for the embellishment of crazy patchwork and, with the exception of the spider's web, all the decorative stitching on the bag illustrated is ribbon embroidery. The use of Australian floral motifs and charms makes the bag a perfect memento of Australia. The same treatment could be applied to a cushion or a jacket.

References to the decorations used in the design are as follows:

1. Kangaroo paw   – page 19
2. Bottle brush   – page 20
3. Gum tree   – page 21
4. Banksia nut   – page 19
5. Initial   – page 31
6. Whipped running stitch – used to apply guipure lace edging.
7. Straight stitch – used to overstitch and further embellish lace edging.
8. Palastrina stitch embellished with beads.
9. Single wrapped straight stitch.
10. Opal cluster – coloured diamantes interspersed with ruched ribbon (page 31) and colonial knots.
11. Earrings (a great use for the odd ones we all end up with), stick pins, lapel tacks, charms and tiny pendants all make great 'do-dads' as they are called in the world of crazy patchwork.

Crazy Patchwork layout — shown half size

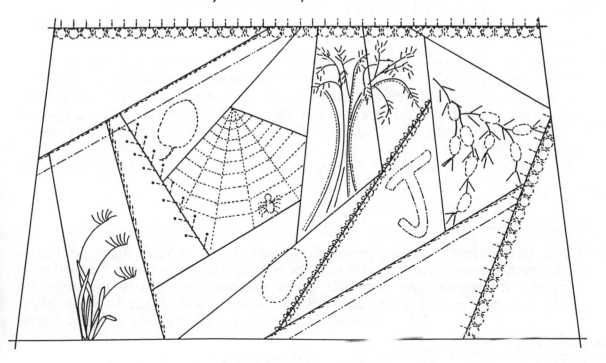

Brooch

Requirements:
Brooch mount
Small piece of lightweight iron-on vilene
2 mm ribbons in required colours

- Using the template provided in the brooch mount kit, mark the outline on the right side of the fabric.
- Centre the design and work carefully, keeping the ribbon as flat as possible on the back of the fabric.
- Press carefully, then back the fabric with iron-on vilene. (The vilene helps to keep the fabric wrinkle-free and prevents the edges from fraying when the shape is cut.)
- Cut out carefully around the marked outline.
- Finish mounting as directed by the manufacturer's instructions.

PERFECT PRESENTATION

Innovative presentation can do a great deal to enhance a gift. There are several examples shown in the illustrated section of this book.

Brooch and Card

A brooch can be put on permanent display if it doubles as the top of a box, as is the case with the tiny kangaroo paw ring box. A brooch pin is sewn to the box top to enable it to be worn. Details of box construction are to be found in *Silk Ribbon Embroidery for Gifts and Garments*.

The embroidered card is designed around the brooch so that the brooch can be displayed as part of the card. The charts for the butterflies are shown on page 30. The design is worked on hardanger 22 evenweave fabric and mounted into a purchased card mount. A piece of wadding, cut to the exact size of the window shape, is inserted between the fabric and the backing sheet of the card to allow the brooch to be pinned to the card easily.

More detailed instructions on making and mounting cards can be found in *Silk Ribbon Embroidery for Gifts and Garments*.

Perforated Paper

Display boxes, cards and small presentation boxes can all be made from perforated paper, which is easy to work with 2 mm silk ribbon. The edges can be finished with whipped stitch worked into each hole. Boxes and containers can be assembled by holding the edges at right angles and working across the join into the corresponding holes on each section. Trim the edges of the paper until they are smooth, before stitching.

The tiny four petal flowers shown on the card and brooch designs have been used to decorate the corner of the tiny purple box. The butterfly earrings displayed on the box are handmade from painted leather.

The lid of the blue box is decorated with a geometric design worked in straight stitch, using two shades of ribbon. Each square is outlined with gold thread.

Embroidered Card and Matching Brooch

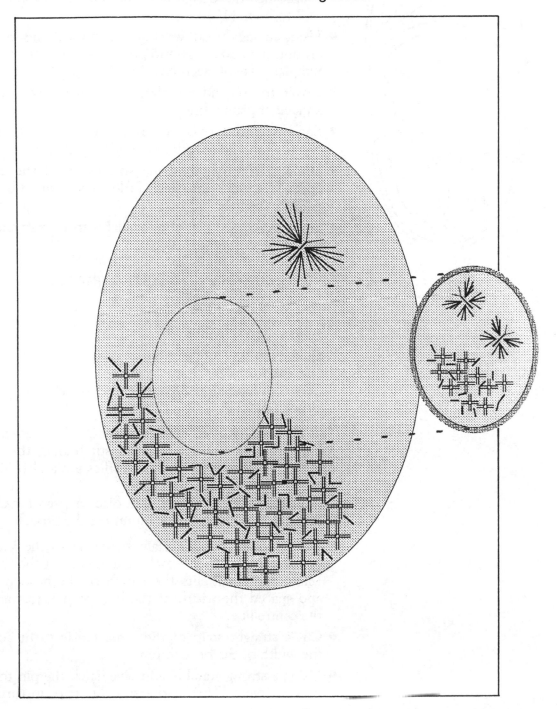

BARETTE

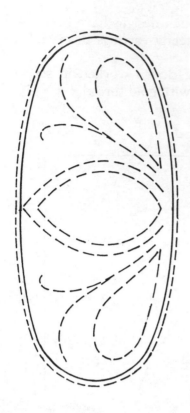

- Make two plastic or cardboard templates from the outline of the design. Copy the complete design on to a sheet of paper. Transfer the design on to the fabric with a thin layer of batting on the back (see page 37).
- Embroider the design and cut out, leaving turnings of 2 to 3 cm (1″).
- Using strong thread, work a row of gathering stitches around the outer edge and pull up to cover the plastic template. Tie off securely.
- Cover the second template in the same way, using a piece of plain fabric.
- Sandwich the two covered pieces wrong sides together and ladder stitch the edges together.
- Work a row of palastrina stitch around the outer edge. Sew beads into each little 'cup' formed by the palastrina stitch.
- Sew a purchased hair clip (available from craft shops) to the back.

INEXPENSIVE IDEAS FOR JEWELLERY

Name Tag or Brooch

(Pictured on the sewing caddy.)

Requirements:
    Porcelain pendant disc
    Scraps of hardanger 22 and leather or felt
    Brooch pin

This design is worked on hardanger 22. The letters are positioned and worked in cross stitch first, then the tiny four petal flowers and butterflies are added in the available space around the name.

An oblong porcelain pendant disc, as used for china painting, forms the base for mounting the brooch.

- Draw around the porcelain shape on to the leather or felt for the brooch backing and cut out the shape. Make two small slits the length of the brooch pin, and spaced the width of the brooch pin, just above the centre line.
- Cut a straight strip of the same fabric to fit across the width of the brooch pin.
- Using a strong suitable adhesive, stick the pin to the backing piece. Thread the straight strip up through

the top slit, across the pin and down through the bottom slit. Glue the ends of the strip firmly to the inside of the backing, clamp and put aside to dry.

- Cut out the embroidered design, leaving ample turnings. Run a gathering thread around and pull the turning to the back of the brooch. Tie off firmly. Trim excess turnings.
- Stick the brooch backing securely in place.
- Work a palastrina knot edging around the edge of the brooch.

Folded Rose Brooches _____

These are lovely little posy brooches, mounted on nothing more expensive than a brass ring!

Requirements:
  Small scraps of silk organza
  Iron-on vilene
  Scrap of fine narrow cotton lace
  Scrap of leather or felt for backing
  3 cm (1¼″) brass ring
  Small brooch pin
  7 mm silk ribbon for roses
  2 mm silk ribbon for leaves

- Draw around the brass ring on to the iron-on vilene, cut out and iron on to a piece of silk organza. The silk organza should be large enough to fit into a small embroidery frame.
- Each brooch requires ten to twelve roses, made as described on page 22. Leave the ribbon ends of each rose long enough to thread into a needle and sew through the vilene-stiffened fabric.
- Arrange the roses into a tight posy. The ends of the ribbons can then be back stitched firmly or sewn to the fabric with thread if you find that easier.
- Add looped straight stitch leaves in 2 mm green ribbon between the flowers.
- Prepare a backing for the brooch, following the instructions given on page 58 for the name brooch and using the brass ring as a template.
- Cut out the brooch, allowing enough turning to gather and pull the fabric to the back of the brass ring.
- Gather the lace into a circle and fit around the outside of the flowers. Sew in place.
- Glue on the backing piece.

CUSHION PANEL

This cushion would make a pretty wedding ring pillow. The heart design can be worked in many different ways; a single heart on a tiny pillow stuffed with pot pourri makes a pretty sachet. The three corner hearts can be used on a collar or yoke or on the front of a purse or lingerie bag.

The hearts are outlined in whipped running stitch. The flower sprays are worked as charted on the pattern.

Cushion Panel

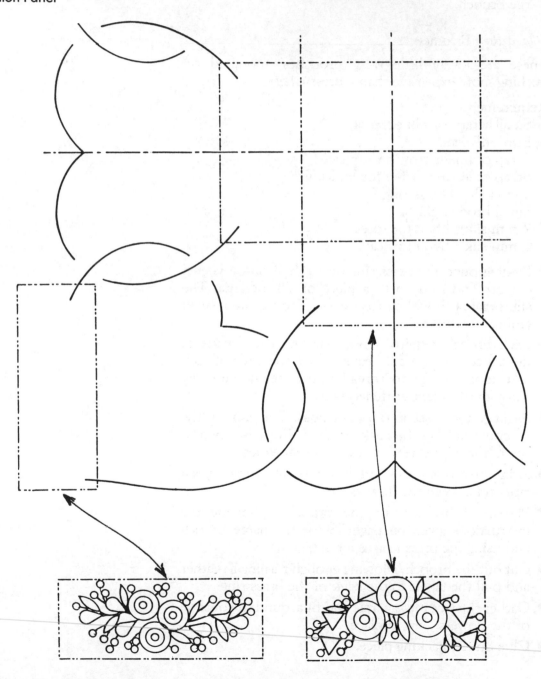

JEWELLERY CADDY

The finished overall size of this caddy is 31 cm x 17 cm
(12¼″ x 6¾″). There are two zip pockets, one open
pocket and a quilted panel on which to pin brooches,
etc. The caddy is made from silk dupion, both inside
and out.

Requirements:
  Fabric   35 cm x 80 cm (14″ x 31½″)
  Pellon   35 cm x 75 cm (14″ x 29½″)
  Two 15 cm (6″) zip fasteners
  35 cm (14″) ribbon or decorative braid,
  approximately 1.5 cm (½″) in width
  50 cm (20″) of 2 or 3 mm (⅛″) wide ribbon for
    ribbon ties
  Decorative button for fastening
  Silk ribbon for embroidery

- Cut the outside panel 35 cm x 18 cm (14″ x 7″).
  Back with pellon and centre the design 8 cm (3″)
  from one end of the panel. Transfer the design as
  detailed on page 37.

- Cut one lining panel 35 cm x 18 cm (14″ x 7″). The
  backing of this panel will depend on the weight of
  the fabric selected for the caddy.

- Cut three pocket pieces and three pellon pieces, each
  15 cm x 18 cm (6″ x 7″). Tack a pellon piece to
  each pocket piece.

- Work all the embroidery, including a flower on each
  pocket piece as shown in the diagram, using a section
  of the design detailed for the knitted vest.

- Fold the pockets in half, wrong sides together, and
  press along the folded edge.

- Lay the zips under the folded edges of two of the
  pockets, allowing the fold to completely cover the
  teeth of the zip. Pin each zip in place *to the lining
  section of the pocket only.* Open out the pocket and
  stitch the zip in place, having the wrong side of the
  zip uppermost as you stitch.

- Fold the pockets again and position on the lining
  panel.

- Use the ribbon or fancy braid to cover the free edge
  of the zip and the bottom of the next pocket. Top
  stitch neatly into place. Repeat for the second zip
  pocket and the base of the third open pocket.

- Cut a piece of fabric and pellon 13 cm x 18 cm
  (5″ x 7″) and quilt (see pages 38-9).

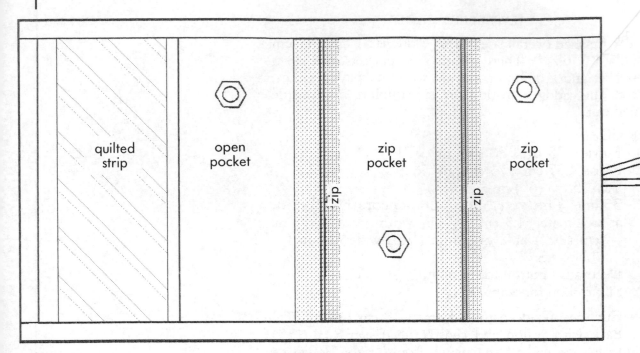

Layout — half size

- Bring the long edges right sides together and sew into a tube.
- Turn inside out, centre the seam at the back and press firmly. Tack into place along the side edges.
- Measure the lining section carefully and trim to size of 31 cm x 18 cm (12″ x 7″). Measure and trim the outer panel to 34 cm x 18 cm (13½″ x 7″). Note that the outer panel is longer than the lining panel.
- Place the two panels right sides together, matching the short ends to each other. Sew across both ends, taking 5 mm (¼″) turnings. Trim the pellon in the seam allowance close to the stitching from the outer panel section only.
- Turn right side out. The extra fabric allowance on the front panel now forms the binding on the ends of the caddy.
- Bind the sides with a straight strip of matching fabric cut double. (See page 38).
- Fold the ribbon tie in half and stitch in place, using two bullion lazy daisy stitches to hold the ribbon loop firmly. Sew a back shank button on the other end close to the fold. Tie the ribbon around the button.

EMBROIDERY CADDY

The sampler makes a great class project and a perfect cover for this caddy.

This useful caddy is designed for the embroidery enthusiast to carry all the requirements needed for the latest project, or to keep packed ready for the next workshop or guild meeting.

It contains large pockets for a clip board, design leaflet, notebook, etc. The spine is strengthened with a metal ruler, a useful piece of equipment, particularly at workshops, and there is ample room for threads, scissors, embroidery hoops, etc.

The finished size of the photographed front panel is 39 cm x 28 cm (15½″ x 11″). This allows for the easy storage of an A4 size clipboard or notebook and most embroidery design leaflets, as well as a 30 cm (12″) ruler in the spine.

The size can be adjusted to suit your own needs. Start your calculations by selecting the length of the zip required for the pockets, which will determine the depth of the caddy. Then adjust the width in proportion to this.

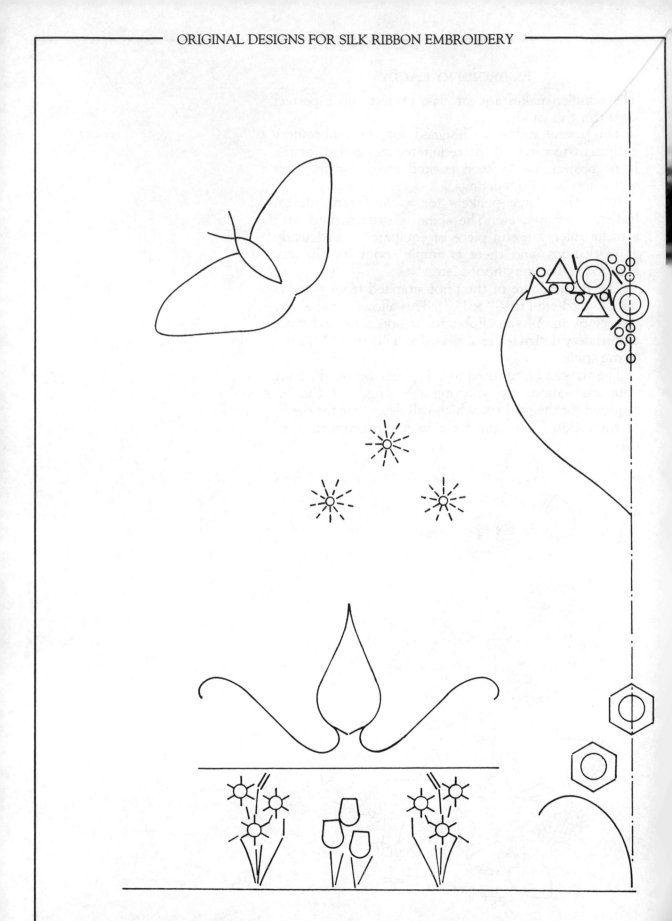

Requirements:
(For the caddy as pictured)

Fabric	1.65 m x 115 cm wide	(1.8 yds x 45″)
Pellon	1.35 m x 90 cm wide	(1.5 yds x 36″)
Cream Aida Band	1.2 m x 5 cm wide	(48″ x 2″)
Lace insertion	1.6 m x 2 cm wide	(63″ x 1″)

(braid or ribbon can be substituted for either of the above two items)

Zips   4, each 35 cm (14″) long

- Cut front panel 65 cm x 39 cm (25½″ x 15½″).

- Cut a pellon backing piece, place the panel and backing together and transfer the required design to the front cover section. Make sure this is positioned correctly so that the folder opens from the right hand side when finished.

- Work the embroidery.

- Quilt the following pieces:
  (Note that the cut size is before quilting and the trimmed size is after quilting. Sizes are in centimetres with inches shown in brackets.)

Item:	Cut Size:	Trimmed Size:
1 backing panel	42 x 68	39 x 65
	(16½″ x 27″)	(15½″ x 25½″)
1 large pocket piece	42 x 62	39 x 59
	(16½″ x 24″)	(15½″ x 23¼″)
2 pocket pieces	42 x 23	39 x 21
	(16½″ x 9″)	(15½″ x 8¼″)

- Cut lining fabric to match the three trimmed quilted pocket pieces.

- Place the lining right sides together with the three pocket pieces. Using a seam allowance of 5 mm (¼″), sew along one long edge of each of the small pocket pieces and along both short edges of the large pocket piece.

- Turn right sides out and press along the machine stitching line.

- Place these finished edges along one side of each of the four zips and top stitch in place. Make sure the zips will open from the left when the pockets are positioned as shown in the diagram.

- Cut two strips of fabric 8 cm wide x 39 cm long (3″ x 15 ½″). Fold each in half along its length and press firmly.

- Place the folded edge along the other side of the zips on the large pocket and sew in place. Decorate these strips with lace insertion.

- Place the smaller pocket pieces on the top of the large section, positioning the centre of the zips 6.5 cm (2½″) away from the centre of the zips on the large pocket. Pin in place.

- Zigzag across the bottom edges of these two pockets.

- Embroider the butterflies, using the charts on page 30, on to the aida band.
- Position a strip of the band to cover the zipper edge and top stitch in place. Top stitch the other edge across the top of the first pocket.
- Use the remaining aida band to make a pocket in the spine.
    - Cut a lining piece to match the remaining aida band and sew right sides together across the top of the band. Fold the lining to the wrong side and position across the middle of the caddy 2.5 cm (1″) down from the top edge. (This edge must not get caught in the binding when finishing the caddy). Trim the lower edge of the band to the lower edge of the caddy.
- Place the whole pocket section on top of the backing section, right sides up.
- Cover the edges of the spine pocket and the other larger pockets with lace insertion or ribbon. Top stitch in place through all thicknesses.
- Make two handles from quilted fabric. Cut two strips each 30 cm long x 5 cm wide (12″ x 2″). Sew into a tube, right sides together. Turn inside out and pin to the sides of the pocket section as indicated on the pattern.
- Place the cover section right sides together with the pocket section and sew across the side edges.
- Turn right sides out, match the top and bottom edges and trim if necessary. Stitch together.
- Cut two straight strips 67 cm x 7 cm (26½″ x 2¾″). Fold in half along the length, press firmly and use to bind the top and bottom edges (see page 38).

Embroidery Caddy Layout

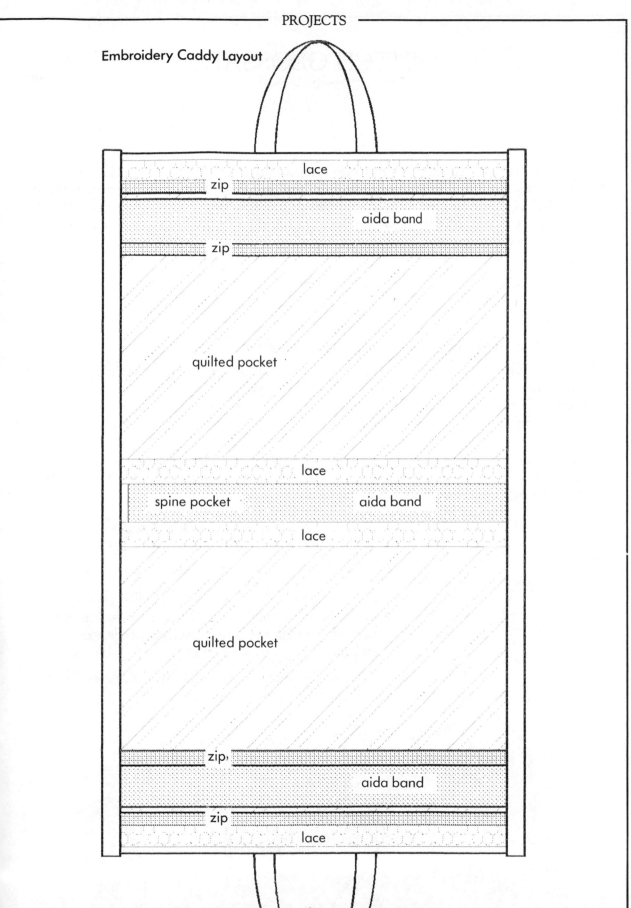

STITCH GLOSSARY

All the stitches used in all my publications on silk ribbon embroidery are listed in this section. The main emphasis given here is to diagrams rather than words. The stitches are described in greater detail in my previous books, to which reference should be made if further information is required. A book reference is included in key form with the stitch heading for each stitch shown in this section, as follows:

Book	Key ref
Silk Ribbon Embroidery: Australian Wildflowers	Bk 1
Silk Ribbon Embroidery 2: Transform Your Clothes	Bk 2
Silk Ribbon Embroidery for Gifts and Garments	Bk 3

Other references included in key form with the stitch headings are:

Washing information	Key ref	Needle recommendation	Key ref
Washable	W	Tapestry	T
Wash with care	W/C	Chenille	Ch
Not washable	NW	Crewel	Cr

On all the applicable diagrams the *odd* numbers refer to the needle passing *up* through the fabric from the back to the front. The *even* numbers refer to the needle passing *down* through the fabric from the front to the back.

BULLION LAZY DAISY AND TWISTED BULLION LAZY DAISY

Bk 1   W   Ch *or* Cr

- Fig 1 & 2 show the normal bullion lazy daisy.
- Fig 3 & 4 show the needle entry position for the second part of the stitch on the other side of the ribbon to give a twisted stitch.

Choose the method of working that gives the best results for the shaping you require.

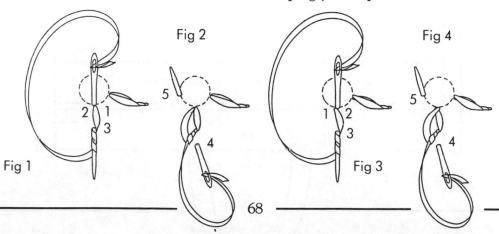

COLONIAL KNOT OR CANDLEWICKING KNOT

Bks 1, 2 & 3   W   Ch *or* Cr

There are different ways of producing these knots and the drawings in the referenced books all have slight variations. However, although the method drawn here is recommended, it is most important that you choose the way you find easiest to produce good knots.

- Fig 1. Ribbon held in the left hand and between the needle and first finger of right hand as the needle is hooked under the ribbon.

- Fig 2. The needle is turned anti-clockwise (left) over the ribbon to hook under the ribbon held by the left hand.

- Fig 3. The needle direction is reversed back over the ribbon and passed to the back of the fabric at point 2.

Not shown, but essential, is to pull down gently on the ribbon held in the left hand, to ensure that the knot is resting on the fabric as the needle is passed through the fabric.

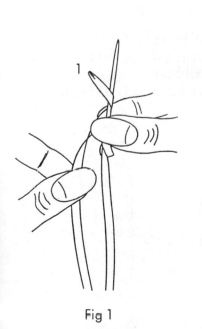

Fig 1

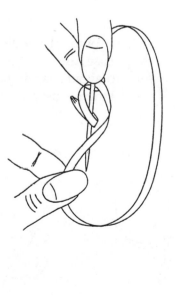

Fig 2

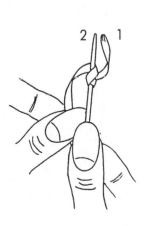

Fig 3

HALF COLONIAL KNOT OR FRENCH KNOT

Bk 3   W   T

- Fig 1. Pick up the ribbon with the needle.
- Fig 2. Turn the needle clockwise over the ribbon held in the left hand. Pass the needle back through the fabric at point 2.

Pull down gently on the ribbon to ensure the knot rests on the fabric as the needle is passed to the back of the work. This is essential for neat compact knots.

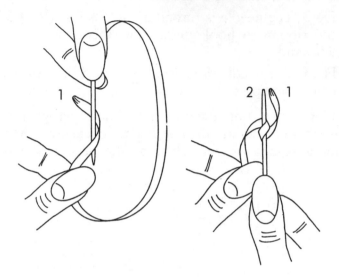

PALASTRINA STITCH OR DOUBLE KNOT STITCH

Bk 2   W   T

A sharp pointed needle can be used for this stitch, in which case the needle is inserted eye first under the stitch to avoid snagging the ribbon.

The stitch is usually worked from left to right.

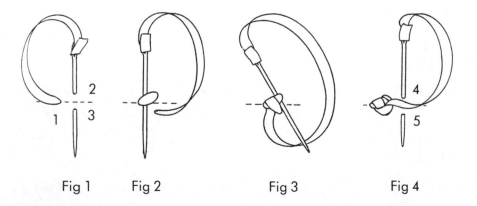

Fig 1   Fig 2   Fig 3   Fig 4

PEARL STITCH

Bk 3   W   T

- Fig 1. Place each vertical stitch across the design line to be followed.
- Fig 2. Keep the ribbon twist free as you tighten the ribbon over the foundation stitch.
- Fig 3. Work from right to left for successive stitches.

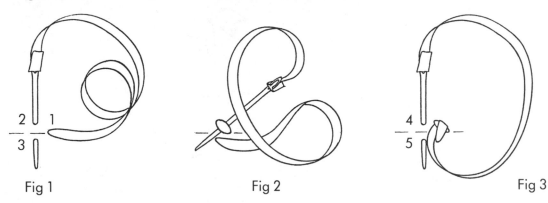

Fig 1   Fig 2   Fig 3

PORTUGUESE STEM STITCH

Bk 2   W   T

- Fig 1. Base stem stitch is laid down.
- Fig 2. First wrap is made with needle above the ribbon.
- Fig 3. Second wrap — needle below the ribbon.
- Fig 4. Second stem stitch.
- Fig 5. First wrap — needle above the ribbon.
- Fig 6. Second wrap — needle below the ribbon and under both stem stitches.

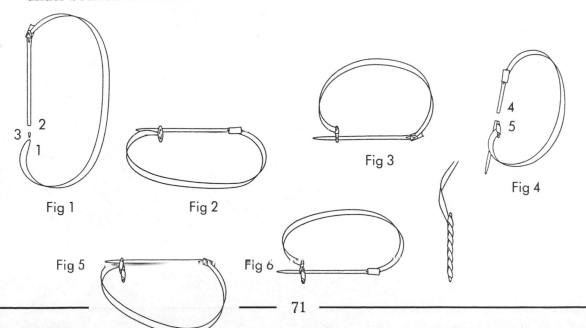

Fig 1   Fig 2   Fig 3   Fig 4

Fig 5   Fig 6

RIBBON STITCH — FLAT

Bk 1   NW   Ch *or* Cr

Always spread the ribbon carefully and pull the ribbon very gently to complete the stitch.

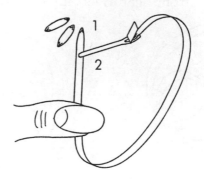

RIBBON STITCH — LOOPED

NW   Ch *or* Cr

A new variation of ribbon stitch.

The needle is passed through the ribbon *only* at the tip of the petal to be formed.

The needle is then passed to the back of the work, 1 to 2 mm ($\frac{1}{16}$″)from point 1.

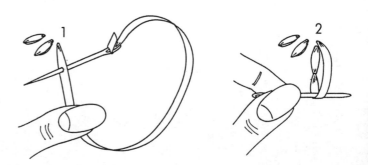

ROSETTE CHAIN

Bk 3   W   T

- Fig 1. After coming up at 1, a small vertical stitch is made to the left of this point, with the ribbon passing over to the left where the stitch is made and back under the point of the needle.
- Fig 2. Stitch is tightened and the needle passed back under the ribbon only.
- Fig 3. Successive stitches are each made to the left of the last stitch. To follow a design line, the vertical stitches are all worked across the line.
- Fig 4. To work individual stitches for buds, pass the needle to the back of the work on completion of step 2.

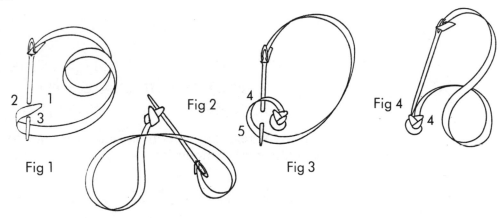

STRAIGHT STITCH — FLAT

Bks 1, 2 & 3   W   Ch *or* Cr

Always spread the ribbon and gently tighten the stitch to the desired tension.

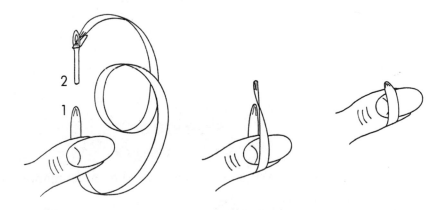

STRAIGHT STITCH — TWISTED

Bk 3   W   Ch *or* Cr

Always spread the ribbon and gently tighten the stitch to the desired tension.

Use matching embroidery thread to anchor the ribbon with a couching thread as you fold the ribbon to change direction.

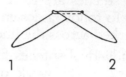

STRAIGHT STITCH — LOOPED

Bk 3   NW   Ch *or* Cr

Always spread the ribbon and take care not to disturb and distort the stitches as you work.

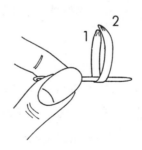

STEM STITCH

W/C   Ch *or* Cr

Spread the ribbon and work in the same manner as for 'Thread Stem Stitch'.

TWISTED CHAIN

Bk 2   W   Ch

- Fig 1. This stitch can be worked from the right or the left, according to the direction you wish the stitch to lay, as shown in the diagrams.
- Fig 2. When working in a continuous line, be sure to keep the needle close to the design line.
- Fig 3. A single twisted chain can be used as a flower petal.

Fig 1   Fig 2   Fig 3

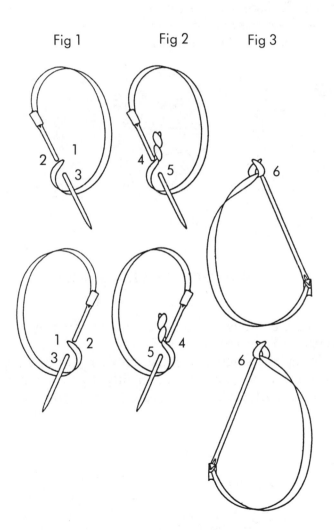

WHIPPED STITCH — RUNNING
Bk 3   W   Cr & T

- Fig 1. A base row of running stitches is worked with a crewel needle. These stitches must be slightly longer than the width of the ribbon used. The distance between stitches should be as small as possible.
- Fig 2. A tapestry needle is used for wrapping. Lay the work down and use both hands on top of the work to manipulate the ribbon. Pass the needle between the running stitches and the fabric, working around each stitch twice.
- Fig 3. Take care to remove all twists each time, by hooking the needle through the loop as you pull the ribbon with the left hand.

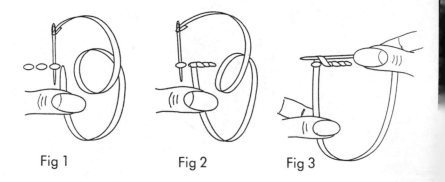

Fig 1   Fig 2   Fig 3

WHIPPED STITCH — SINGLE
Bk 3   W   T

Pay careful attention to the comments for the 'running' version of this stitch.

Wrap the single straight stitch with five or six wraps or until it is covered sufficiently for your purpose. Always work pulling the needle towards you.

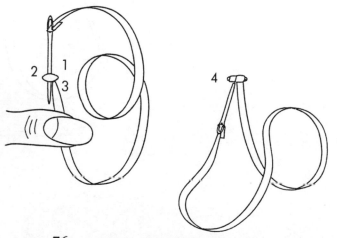

THREAD STITCHES

COUCHING

Bks 1, 2 & 3

The use of two needles, one to lay the main thread and the other to stitch it down, gives greater flexibility for shaping.

BULLION STITCH

Bk 1 (See also my *Bullion Stitch Embroidery* book)

Use a straw needle. Silk thread, a shiny thread, is easier for working this stitch than a thread with a dull finish.

FEATHER STITCH

Bk 3

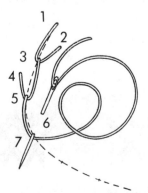

LADDER STITCH
Bk 3

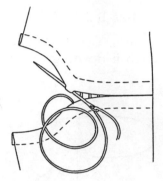

LAZY DAISY STITCH
Bk 2

MODIFIED LAZY DAISY STITCH
Bk 1

PADDED HERRINGBONE STITCH

This stitch is formed by working three layers of close herringbone stitch, each layer completely covering the stitching of the previous row.

PISTIL STITCH
Bk 1

SATIN STITCH
Bk 2

STEM STITCH

Any queries for the author should be directed to:
Jenny Bradford
7 Noala Street
Aranda ACT 2614
Australia
Phone: (06) 254 6814